SINGER

PETER FLANNERY

Peter Flannery studied drama at Manchester University before joining Contact Theatre there and writing his first play for them, *Heartbreak Hotel* (1975). There followed *Last Resort* (Sidewalk Theatre Company, 1976; Royal Exchange, Manchester, 1978), *The Boy's Own Story* (Rat Theatre Company, 1978), *Savage Amusement* and *Awful Knawful*, a play for children co-written with Mick Ford (both staged at the RSC Warehouse in 1978). From 1979–80 he was Writer in Residence at the Royal Shakespeare Company in London, for whom he wrote *Our Friends in the North* (1982), which won the John Whiting Award that year. His five-part series, *Blind Justice*, was shown on BBC-TV in 1988, winning the Royal Television Society Award and the Samuel Beckett Award.

PETER FLANNERY

SINGER

NICK HERN BOOKS

A division of Walker Books Limited

A Nick Hern Book

Singer first published in 1989 as an original paperback by
Nick Hern Books, a division of Walker Books Limited,
87 Vauxhall Walk, London SE11 5HJ

Front cover illustration: *Singer* by Antony Sher, reproduced by
courtesy of the artist

Set in Baskerville by Book Ens, Saffron Walden, Essex
Printed by Richard Clay Ltd, Bungay, Suffolk

British Library Cataloguing in Publication Data
Flannery, Peter
    Singer.
    I. Title
    822'.914

    ISBN 1-85459-066-9

Caution

SINGER

Singer was first staged by the Royal Shakespeare Company at the Swan Theatre, Stratford-upon-Avon.

First preview was 27 September 1989; press night was 11 October 1989.

The cast was as follows:

REFUGEE/SECRETARY/TWIN/ SERVANT/ELLIE/VAGRANT	Lucy Ellis
FIRED SERVANT/RUBY	Amanda Harris
FROI RINGELBAUM/REFUGEE/ MRS DALEY/VAGRANT	Helena McCarthy
REFUGEE/GLORIA/LADY BUNTY/ WOMAN AT SOUTH BANK	Jane Maud
WEST INDIAN MOTHER/SERVANT/ JANICE/VAGRANT	Clara Onyemere
REFUGEE/MARIA/TWIN/LADY BASIL/DENISE	Cassie Stuart
NCO 1/PEPPER/DEREK/TIM BUNTY	Alan Cumming
GAILUNAS/HARTY/DE KNOP	Russell Dixon
STEFAN	Mick Ford
MUSSELMAN/REFUGEE/ MR DALEY/SIR BASIL/VAGRANT	Eric Francis
NCO 2/PHOTOGRAPHER/ SERVANT/COLIN/VAGRANT	Adrian Hilton
REFUGEE/LORD BUNTY/VAGRANT	George Malpas
CHORUS/IMMIGRATION OFFICER/ CONSTABLE/BUTLER/CHORUS AS VAGRANT	Joe Melia
2ND KAPO/REFUGEE/BLYTHE/ POLICEMAN/ALMOND	Harry Miller
REFUGEE/LORD EARNER/ VAGRANT	Jo O'Conor
3RD KAPO/REFUGEE/MILLER/ POLICEMAN/CURBISHLEY	Craig Pinder
WEST INDIAN FATHER/SERVANT/ PAUL/VAGRANT	Ade Sapara

PETER SINGER	Antony Sher
MANIK	Malcolm Storry
1ST KAPO/REFUGEE/SCHOFIELD/ POLICEMAN/DAWSON	} Peter Theedom
ZEBRA/REFUGEE/SHALLCROSS/ MAN FROM THE MINISTRY	} Mark Williams
WEST INDIAN CHILD	Solomon Onyemere

Directed by Terry Hands
Designed by Sanja Jurca Avci
Assistant Director Ruth Garnault
Stage Manager Michael Dembowicz
Deputy Stage Manager Neil Constable
Assistant Stage Manager Ian Morgan-James

This text went to press before the opening night, and may therefore differ slightly from the text as performed.

PROLOGUE

Auschwitz Central.

Enter CHORUS.

CHORUS. If we had all night and day and a hundred performers
and an army of stage crew to take off the Polish Vienna and
bring on Notting Hill, fly away Auschwitz Central by day and
wheel on Clapham Junction by night, and if we had a
thousand costumes and make-up artists who could perform
miracles with likenesses, we still could not give you all the
fantastical comedy of The Life of Singer. But let's begin.
Remember. Remember: a time, and what a time, when war
was not a crime but a crusade. Not a television war we
couldn't understand with napalm or nerve gas killing Asian
strangers but an everyday reality with TNT igniting in our own
streets, dropping into our own living-rooms, a different kind of
carpet bombing altogether. If we had a sky to fill with dark
and light we'd paint up memories of a war that didn't baffle us
– like later, littler wars – or bore us stiff to tell the truth or split
us into camps of 'yes' or 'no' or 'I dunno' but pressed our
million little lives into one big idea: Freedom. Freedom to
keep things how they'd always been: to holiday on beaches in
the rain and keep our bad teeth and laughing policemen.
Freedom to ignore each other gently, and every man be left in
peace dictating terms to no one but himself. Let other nations
sell their souls for drums and torches and loyalty parades, little
England stands alone and fights like a lion for the right to
believe what we'd always believed: that foreigners are born
funny and nothing in the world will ever change. But
everything has changed already.

Enter ZEBRAS, BLOCKCHIEFS, KAPOS. *This is a corner of the
laager where a market usually happens. But today there is no market.*

CHORUS. The world we fought for was killed in action. The
battleground a place we never heard of yet. There was gas.
There were strangers. And they were working too. For
freedom. Arbeit macht frei. Zebras. Blockchiefs. Kapos. And

those about to step out of life and into everlasting rest: musselmen. Criminal. Political. Jew. In a world of black and white.

SINGER *enters and walks forward at a snail's pace. He walks like a man already half out of existence.*

SINGER. Cold. Cold. Cold.

CHORUS. If we had another sky to fill with charcoal and hang it close enough to touch. If we had a million lonely skeletons to stamp their frozen feet on the cold earth, we still could not give you this place, as it really was. But we'll do our best with what we have and let imagination do the rest.

Exit CHORUS.

The KAPOS *taunt* SINGER.

1ST KAPO. Singer. Singer.

2ND KAPO. Musselman, can you hear it? Another winter coming.

SINGER (*to the audience*). Not for me. I had that dream again last night. I'm sitting at dinner with friends – still wearing these pyjamas. The table is piled high with food and all my best friends and my dear mother and father are with me. I try to eat but somehow I cannot get the food into my mouth. I am starving but I cannot get the food into my mouth. My mother asks me why I don't eat. 'Aren't you hungry, Peter?' I try to tell her, 'I'm so hungry'. I try to tell them where I've been; I try to tell them this is real; it can't be, but it is; it's really happening to me: Peter Singer, who was going to be a dentist. They seem embarrassed and talk among themselves. Because they can't hear me. I talk louder but they don't listen. My mother and father won't listen. In my dream I wake from a dream. And I know why they didn't need to listen. They already knew the story of this place. Because they've been here before me. Been and gone. Where's the market?

1ST KAPO. No market today.

SINGER. But I need soup. I have a coupon. Won't somebody take my coupon?

2ND KAPO. What good are coupons now? There's not a shred of tobacco to back them up. The market's collapsed.

SINGER. I have to have soup.

2ND KAPO. Give me your shirt and I can get you half a bowl of soup.

SINGER *thinks about it. Snowflakes fall.*

SINGER. It's so cold. Look: the first snowflakes. Another winter on the way.

1ST KAPO. Not for you. Why not eat?

SINGER *takes off his shirt and hands it over. He holds out his bowl. 1ST KAPO pours him half of his bowl of soup. STEFAN comes on, a fair-haired, blue-eyed boy, fifteen years old.*

STEFAN. Uncle Peter, what are you doing?

SINGER. I had to have soup.

SINGER *is about to devour it.*

STEFAN. Don't eat it. Offer it back to the kapos. Get coupons.

SINGER. Coupons?

He tries to eat it. STEFAN *prevents it.*

STEFAN. As many as you can.

SINGER. Coupons are worthless.

STEFAN. Now they are worthless; by tonight it will be different. Gailunas is going to make an announcement. But we must be quick. Uncle Peter, this is your chance.

GAILUNAS *enters, a Ukrainian camp guard.*

(*To* SINGER.) Wait. Don't drink it.

STEFAN *goes to* GAILUNAS.

Sir, five minutes before you make your announcement please, I humbly request.

SINGER *picks up the soup and lets the bowl warm his hands.*

Peter, wait!

He goes back to GAILUNAS.

Give me five minutes and tonight I will bring you a girl.

SINGER *smells the soup.*

Wait, Uncle Peter!

SINGER *moves the soup away from his mouth.*

GAILUNAS *walks away.*

STEFAN *follows him.*

Two girls. Sisters. Uncle Peter!

GAILUNAS *turns back to* STEFAN.

Twins. Identical twins. Virgins.

GAILUNAS. How do you know they're virgins?

STEFAN. They come from the Children's Block.

GAILUNAS. Five minutes.

SINGER *drinks the soup.*

GAILUNAS *leaves.*

SINGER *puts the bowl on the ground.*

STEFAN *sees what he's done.*

STEFAN. What have you done?

SINGER *remains silent. Defeated, he lies down.*

STEFAN *cleans* SINGER'*s bowl and looks at it.*

You've got five minutes. Get up. Are you going to let them select you? So tomorrow you will go up the chimney, where your family went before; and mine; and I'll go as well. Yes?

SINGER *cries.*

STEFAN *gets angry.*

Get up. Get up. You are all I have. Get up! I gave Gailunas two children so that you would have time to get coupons! Uncle Peter! Don't die! Please!

SINGER *stands unsteadily.*

Give them your bowl and spoon; and mine. Give them mine. Give them my shirt.

STEFAN *hands* SINGER *his own bowl and spoon.*

SINGER. Are you sure about coupons? What if you're wrong?

STEFAN. Then we're both dead, Uncle Peter. No more cold; no more beatings; no more sending children to the gas. No more do I have to choose which ones die today and which tomorrow.

STEFAN *takes off his shirt and buttons up his jacket to conceal the absence.* SINGER *goes to market with their belongings.*

(To the audience.) And will any one of us remain alive at the end? Oh God: I hope not. We'll all be whipped along the road to heaven; two thousand six hundred and eighty-one children will be waiting there for me and *they* will sit in judgement on *me.*

1ST KAPO. Coupons? He's finally gone mad. Here take as many coupons as you want.

The other KAPOS *laugh as they exchange the belongings for coupons.* SINGER *comes back.*

SINGER. Now what?

STEFAN. We wait.

They pray silently.

GAILUNAS *comes back in. He walks slowly around.*

SINGER. They can hang us if we have no shirt.

They continue praying.

GAILUNAS *addresses the other* KAPOS.

GAILUNAS. Tonight, there will be a fresh consignment of Polish females. Kapos and civilian workers will be allowed to partake, provided they have some coupons.

GAILUNAS *leaves.*

SINGER *and* STEFAN *cheer and praise God. The* KAPOS *besiege them; they trade back their belongings, plus some bread, utensils, a little tobacco and paper.*

SINGER. I thought you said there was no tobacco in the camp?

They go on trading: a spare shirt, a pair of shoes, a homemade lighter, some soap, a razor blade . . .

3RD KAPO. An extra bowl of soup for fourteen days.

SINGER. Each.

3RD KAPO. Each.

And still they have some coupons left over.

2ND KAPO. You are a shrewd bastard, Singer.

SINGER. I know how to drive a bargain.

1ST KAPO. I thought you were finished.

SINGER. It's all a question of timing.

3RD KAPO. You had everybody fooled.

SINGER. Including myself.

SINGER *gnaws the bread.*

There's always another day, Stefan. Make a deal today and live until tomorrow. That's the important thing.

STEFAN *starts to leave.*

Thank you; thank you.

MANIK *comes on. He's a German political prisoner, a Gentile.*

(*Aside.*) Ah! Here comes a high number; only been here a week and one foot already in the grave.

MANIK *wears a red triangle denoting a political prisoner. He stands for a while before announcing apologetically:*

MANIK (*to* SINGER). I'm starving, comrade.

SINGER. Yes, yes, everybody's starving.

MANIK. Is this the market?

SINGER. What have you got?

MANIK. A coupon. I gave my spoon for it yesterday. But it is worthless. I was cheated. Nobody wants coupons.

SINGER. No. Completely worthless.

STEFAN. Uncle Peter . . .

SINGER. Never again, Stefan; ever. Besides, look, red triangle, not one of us, political, communist.

MANIK. I dreamt all night of dumplings. I woke up with the taste of real dumplings in my mouth. But nothing in my belly. My stomach thinks my throat is cut. One bite of bread, comrade.

SINGER *thinks.*

SINGER. Believe me, comrade, I understand hunger. You can

have the whole piece for the coupon – and your shirt: you're a bull of a man, you don't need a shirt.

MANIK. But it's an offence.

SINGER *(aside)*. A high number, but he's learning quick. *(To* MANIK.) That's your problem, not mine. It's not an offence to have two shirts.

STEFAN. Or three? Or four?

SINGER. Or five or six. Well, is it?

STEFAN *looks away*.

(To MANIK.) Nobody's forcing you – make up your mind.

MANIK *takes off his shirt. The deal is done.* MANIK *gnaws at his bread.*

GAILUNAS *comes on, watching.*

Other ZEBRAS *are approaching, slowly, drawn by the comforting spectacle of someone else's suffering.*

GAILUNAS. Where is your shirt? Shirt.

STEFAN. He's a high number; he's German –

GAILUNAS. Quiet, Jew.

STEFAN. He doesn't understand Polish yet –

GAILUNAS *lashes out at* STEFAN *and catches him across the arm.*

STEFAN *is quiet.*

GAILUNAS. Where is your shirt?

MANIK *now understands.*

MANIK. Shirt? I gave it to that bastard over there.

GAILUNAS. What's this shit he's saying?

SINGER. He says he lost it, boss. He's very sorry. He's a high number – he may have taken his eye off it in the washroom –

But GAILUNAS *has already struck* MANIK *a sickening blow to the head and turns on* SINGER.

GAILUNAS. Shut up, you piece of Jewish shit. What are you?

SINGER. A piece of Jewish shit. I humbly request permission to go back to my block –

MANIK, *who has remained standing, though stunned, now begins to moan.*

GAILUNAS *hits him again on the head.*

SINGER. Ah!

STEFAN. Fall down.

But MANIK *stays on his feet, completely disorientated.*

GAILUNAS *turns back to* SINGER.

GAILUNAS. You are not even shit. You are less than shit. Do you know why you are here?

SINGER. No.

GAILUNAS. Because you are worth less than this piece of shit on my boots and that is a fact of life. It is *the* fact of life. It's all you need to know about yourself anymore. What are you?

SINGER. Worthless. I'm nothing. I'm not worth hitting, I humbly suggest.

GAILUNAS. Take it off.

SINGER *picks the piece of shit off the bottom of* GAILUNAS's *boot.*

MANIK's *moans have turned to screams as he clutches his damaged head and sinks to the floor.*

GAILUNAS *beats* MANIK *some more. He turns back to* SINGER.

Eat it.

SINGER *obeys instantly.*

GAILUNAS. Hit him, you hit him.

SINGER *obeys.*

Hit him, again, harder, harder.

They beat MANIK *hard. They stop.*

GAILUNAS *leaves.*

The ZEBRAS *leave slowly, zombie-like.*

STEFAN *helps* MANIK *to his feet.*

MANIK *is very badly hurt but conscious.*

Slowly, they make their way off.

The CHORUS *returns, passing through them as we move to . . .*

ACT ONE

Scene One

Southampton Docks.

Winter. Cold. Fog. Fog horns. Men are disembarking from a freighter.

An army band plays quietly.

CHORUS. Now there is a seam in indivisible humanity, for some
were there and some were not. How will those who saw it
speak to those who did not? Where are the words to describe
what's true but must not be believed – when to believe it (just
believe it) is to lose the gist of your own little humanity? And
who had the stomach for more of death when now at last the
skies were empty and the streets were full of parties? Dads
came home from foreign shores, Mums from factories and
farms, and kids gave up fresh air for good and came back to
the cities – all clear that in the wastelands and the bombsites
would grow a new England, earned in sacrifice and clinched by
victory. Never again would England belong to people who
could drive to the country when the bombs started dropping.
But wars cost money – and the bill was soon delivered. Back to
England then, with the parties dead and gone and only grass
growing on the bombsites. Battered, exhausted England.
Victorious in ruins. Imperial still, but bankrupt. Grey, drawn,
but to those who suffered – and now have dreams of forgetting
– still England: cold harbour paradise.

Carrying cardboard suitcases, refugees disembark from the freighter.
Among them are SINGER, STEFAN *and* MANIK.

They are met by IMMIGRATION OFFICIALS *with paperwork and*
questions.

The BAND *is tired. The music peters out.*

The BAND *sits silently.*

An OFFICIAL *confronts them.*

IMMIGRATION OFFICIAL. Does any of you speak English?

Most of them look at him uncomprehending.

STEFAN. Say words. Little words.

SINGER. My daughter!
   Oh my duck's hat!
   Fled with a Christian!
   Oh my duck's hat and my daughter!
   William Shakespeare.

IMMIGRATION OFFICIAL. Ah! Well, look, try to listen carefully
   to what I'm saying; you may be expecting to simply walk off
   the docks and into normal life here in England.

   MANIK *raises his hand.*

Yes?

MANIK. California ist einer grosser Fische.

IMMIGRATION OFFICIAL. I'm sorry.

MANIK. California . . . is a big fish.

IMMIGRATION OFFICIAL. Yes. This is England. You were
   expecting England, weren't you?

MANIK. California ist einer grosser Fische, das unts verschlukt.

   MANIK *makes a big gulp. The others think he's barely sane.*

IMMIGRATION OFFICIAL. I'm sorry.

MANIK. I'm in the groove, Joe.

SINGER. He's 'meshuge'. Hit head. 'Meshuge.'

IMMIGRATION OFFICIAL. Ah! Is he now?

   IMMIGRATION OFFICIAL *looks at his paperwork, to see if there is
   any note of this.*

   (*To* MANIK.) You are . . . ?

STEFAN. He's with us. He go with us. Us.

IMMIGRATION OFFICIAL. Well some of you will be going to
   Slough initially. Slough.

REFUGEES. (*Muttering*) Slow. Slow.

IMMIGRATION OFFICIAL. Into a camp. Until we can sort you
   out; and others to Kirkcudbright.

ALL. Das laager.

MANIK. When does the sun come out, for fuck's sake?

The OTHERS *shush him, but it's true, they're perishingly cold and without the benefit of the* OFFICIAL'*s topcoat.*

SINGER. If they find out you're a communist you will be back on the boat.

IMMIGRATION OFFICIAL. Now listen to me. I am going to give you some advice. Forget: forget the past. You've had terrible experiences. But there is nothing to be gained by dwelling on the past. The future's what counts; you must make up your minds who and what you want to be.

STEFAN. We are Jews. Polish Jews.

IMMIGRATION OFFICIAL. Then I should tell you this. There are Polish support groups but they're not terribly keen on Jews; and there are Jewish support groups but they're not terribly keen on Poles.

SINGER. We'll forget. We all want be English. God save the King!

REFUGEES. (*Muttering*) God save the King.

SINGER (*proclaiming*).
The King's a dirty shoe!
I kiss his ballcock
and a heart of gold!

IMMIGRATION OFFICIAL. I'm afraid you'll find that pushing yourself to the front of the queue is rather frowned upon in this country. I want all your names. Then I want two queues. I want Slough in a line here and Kirkcudbright here. Understand?

They form groups.

SINGER. This is the queue for Slough. In England you have to queue.

STEFAN *remains alone.*

SINGER *goes to him.*

Come on, get in line. We want to get the best seats at the front of the bus. Whoever's at the front gets off first. Whoever gets off first gets the pick of the beds. I chose Slough; I can't say the other word.

STEFAN. I don't want to be told: forget. Nobody should forget; we should all sit down now and write down everything that has happened. Don't you see?

SINGER. No.

STEFAN. Uncle Peter.

SINGER (*angrily*). What did you keep me alive for? Just to keep me in the camps forever? No.

STEFAN. Are we supposed to forget also what was taken from us? Is Slough like Lvov?

SINGER. Lvov doesn't exist anymore. That life is over.

STEFAN. I only have one life.

SINGER. It won't be enough.

MANIK. Wo ist mein Koffer?

MANIK *is in an argument with some of the others about his suitcase, which he has misplaced. He starts attacking them.*

MANIK. Welcher verdammte Dieb hat meinen Koffer geklaut? Hier gibts nur Diebe! Du? Du? Du? Ich bin nicht blod. Ich kriege meinen Koffer wieder. Ihr seit alle verücht? Ihr Klaut von mir. Ihr nehmt mir alles Weck und glaubt ich marke das nicht.

SINGER *sorts it out.*

They line up.

SINGER *and* MANIK *are at the front of the queue for Slough.*

STEFAN *stands apart.*

The OFFICIAL *notices* STEFAN.

IMMIGRATION OFFICIAL. Well? Now Corporals, Slough that way, Kirkcudbright that way. Carry on, Corporals.

SINGER. Stefan. Here. I've saved a place for you.

STEFAN *joins the line for Kirkcudbright.*

The BAND *starts to play.*

The REFUGEES *trudge off with their belongings.*

IMMIGRATION OFFICIAL. Slough.

SINGER. Stefan? Stefan? Stefan?

SINGER's *group is marched off to a quicker tempo as the* BAND *strikes a lighter note. The scene begins to change with a little more colour now.*

But SINGER *stands and watches* STEFAN *go, and has to be called upon several times to get in line with the other marchers. It's noticeable that* MANIK *never leaves his side.*

Scene Two

A street in Bayswater

A sunny afternoon.

A telephone box.

A family of West Indian immigrants with all their worldly belongings in suitcases. FATHER, MOTHER, CHILD. *The* FATHER *is reading the 'Accommodation to let' advertisements in the evening paper.*

A very well-dressed young woman is waiting for someone; this is MARIA, *aged eighteen.*

Above, an open window in a tenement block. From it is coming loud recorded opera music. SINGER *is joining in. So, unfortunately, is* MANIK.

In the telephone box the phone starts ringing. After a while the West Indian FATHER *wonders whether to answer it.*

The music stops.

SINGER (*off, above*). I'm coming, I'm coming.

   The FATHER *opens the door of the telephone box.*

   SINGER *runs on. He reprimands the* FATHER.

   A – a – a!

   The FATHER *goes back to his family.*

   SINGER *collects his thoughts, waits a beat, puts his hand through an empty pane and picks up the phone.*

Good afternoon. Peter Singer Enterprises. Mr Singer speaking. Hello, Mr O'Brian. What? No, I was dealing with a client in the outer office. Now, Mr O'Brian, Harry, I'll tell you what it

was. Just by chance this could be your lucky day. You must
have been to Mass this morning, eh? Said a few 'Hail Mary's'.
Yes, I'm getting to the point. You're a busy man?

Don't talk to me about busy, Harry, I'm rushed off my feet;
you should see my desk. Just a second, Harry.

MANIK *has followed him on.*

SINGER *addresses the next piece to him.*

Miss Bellhatchet, have you finished those letters? Oh, please
hurry Miss Bellhatchet.

MANIK *looks blank.*

SINGER *talks into the phone again.*

Sorry; this new secretary; she's one of these 'debs', Harry. I
took her on as a favour to her father; he's a baronet or
something. Anyway the thing is, Harry, I can do you a
fabulous deal in a dozen gross 15 denier ladies stockings. No,
no, listen, what about some frying pans . . .? Hello?

O'BRIAN *has hung up.*

SINGER *replaces the phone, quietly cursing and making notes in a
book.*

Enter FROI RINGELBAUM, *an elderly Jewish lady.*

SINGER (*in Polish*). Dog's blood! Cholera! Cunt!

(*Then, in Yiddish:*)

Froi Ringelbaum, Froi Ringelbaum, do I have a nice watch for
you!

FROI RINGELBAUM. I don't want it.

SINGER. Look at it, Froi Ringelbaum, isn't it nice?

But she has gone again.

God protect us from Irish businessmen. If I had lightbulbs,
the sun would never set.

What are you looking at?

The WEST INDIAN FAMILY *is gawping at him.*

WEST INDIAN FATHER. I'm waiting for the phone.

SINGER. No, no, no, no, no, no, no, no. You've just arrived, haven't *you?* You see in this country we all have our own phones. This is a business line. This is *my* phone. *Your* phone is round the corner. You'll soon get the hang of it. Manik, what's wrong?

MANIK. Uncle Peter, the sheepskin stinks.

SINGER. *Don't.* I know all about the sheepskin.

MANIK. But . . .

SINGER. Manik, are we hungry?

MANIK. No.

SINGER. Is anybody beating us?

MANIK. No.

SINGER. Then don't *worry.* Nothing *matters.*

SINGER *sees* MARIA.

Oy! Oy! Look at *that.* Isn't she *beautiful?* Do you think she is on the game?

MANIK. In such a dress?

SINGER. Don't be deceived by appearances. I'll ask her.

SINGER *consults his watch.*

(*To* MANIK.) Keep people out of the phone box; I'm expecting a call.

The WEST INDIAN FATHER *goes off in search of a phone. The* FAMILY *stays.*

SINGER *approaches* MARIA.

Excuse me, madam, this gentleman and I couldn't help noticing your unearthly beauty. If you are on the game, we would both be interested. Otherwise, what about supper one evening this week? We have an apartment just here. (*He points up above.*) It's not exactly a penthouse suite but it has some rather amusing features.

GLORIA *arrives.*

GLORIA. Like a hundredweight of uncured sheepskin in the bath!

SINGER. Gloria!

GLORIA. Peter, this is my kid *sister* for God's sake.

SINGER (*to* MANIK). There, I told you she was on the game.

GLORIA. Maria, this is Peter Singer.

SINGER. 'Maria'! (*Singing.*) 'Oy vey, Maria.'

MARIA. This is him? Is he Jewish or something?

SINGER. Jewish? Are dumplings in a dream really dumplings? I'm a Pole, Maria.

We're very clean, Maria, if you know what I mean. It's the circumcision. We're not like these dirty, unwashed Englishmen – you pull back their foreskins and dragonflies come out.

The phone rings. GLORIA *goes to answer it.*

SINGER *turns to* MARIA.

Have you thought about my offer? Think about a price. You've got fabulous teeth. May I?

GLORIA *answers the phone.*

GLORIA. Good afternoon; Peter Singer Enterprises; hold the line please. (*She pauses.*) Hello? I'm afraid Mr Singer's in a very important meeting, can I take a message?

SINGER *is examining* MARIA's *teeth. She succumbs to his charms.*

GLORIA. Oh! Mr Grunfeld.

MANIK. Grunfeld.

GLORIA. Mr Singer did say that if *you* rang I was to interrupt his meeting. Could you please hold a second?

SINGER. Manik, show Maria the apartment.

MARIA *and* MANIK *leave the stage as* SINGER *squeezes in the phone box with* GLORIA.

Issie! How's business? How's the family? Yes. Just hold it one second, Issie, something big's come up.

He covers the phone.

Gloria? How about a quick ten bob? It's that sister of yours . . . she's got me going.

GLORIA *scans the road and squeezes back into the phone box.*

Issie, where were we? Oh yes, the sheepskin. What do you

mean, 'what sheepskin'? *Your* sheepskin, the sheepskin that's in my bath. The neighbours are complaining, it wouldn't be so bad if the weather wasn't so hot.

GLORIA *has pulled down* SINGER's *trousers and is crouching in front of him.*

The WEST INDIAN MOTHER *can't stand any more.*

WEST INDIAN MOTHER. That's it; we're going back to Trinidad. Come on.

She marches her curious CHILDREN *off in a line.*

SINGER. *Now please* explain, Issie. No, I'm not in a hurry. Ah ah? Ah ah? Oh! Oh! Well of course I sound angry. What am I supposed to do with a hundredweight of uncured sheepskin?

SINGER *comes. He drops the phone.*

Argh!

GLORIA *pulls up his trousers.*

Hello?

ISSIE *has hung up.* SINGER *replaces the telephone.*

They come out of the phone box and sit on the wall.

SINGER *sighs heavily. He fishes out a ten shilling note and hands it to* GLORIA.

Gloria, I think I'm in love with your sister. Do you think she would agree to be my mistress as well?

GLORIA. You can't afford another mistress, Peter. You can hardly afford *me.*

SINGER *knows that this is true; he is dejected.*

Peter, what happened to all that ambition? When I first met you, you were going to do so much. A million pounds. A Rolls Royce. Hampstead Mansion. A knighthood.

SINGER. Psh . . . knighthood! They won't even give me citizenship. I'm not good enough to be British.

GLORIA. Why are you messing about with frying pans and dud watches? You've got a talent.

SINGER. Talent? I've got nothing. I'm nothing here. You're welcome in this country as long as you want to work like a nigger but if you want to build up your own business, forget it!

GLORIA. You need a good woman.

SINGER. I need a good idea. Something *they* didn't think of first.

GLORIA. Peter, you're as good as any of them. I should know.
(*She tries to take his hand.*)

SINGER. What do you know about what I am? That's what I am;
there. (*He shows his tattoo.*) What right have you to criticise me?
You're so good at business? 'I should know'! Who are you
trying to kid?

She touches his shoulder tenderly.

GLORIA. Peter . . .

He shrugs her off, repelled.

SINGER. What? Don't touch me.

GLORIA. You can have these things removed. You could grow
back your hair.

SINGER. Thank you for your advice. I believe you've been paid.

This hurts her.

GLORIA. To hell with you then.

SINGER. Gladly. With all my heart.

GLORIA. You've left three dozen frying pans in my bath; I want
them out by Friday, or I'll give them away free – one to every
satisfied customer.

SINGER. It would take you till Christmas!

GLORIA. So we're finished, are we? Peter? Are you sure?

SINGER. Go and find someone else to criticise.

GLORIA. You know you don't like being alone.

SINGER. Everybody's alone.

She gets up to go.

MARIA *comes on, followed by* MANIK.

MANIK. Warum schreist Du mich an? Ich wollte nur mit Dir
reden und mich um Dich Kümmern. Warum wirst Du so
wild?

MARIA. Apartment? Call that an apartment? What a stink! And

who is this? It's like trying to have a conversation with something from the lagoon.

GLORIA. She doesn't mean it, Manik. Manik!

MANIK *rips the door off the phone box. Then he advances on* MARIA *threateningly.*

SINGER *(quietly)*. Manik.

MANIK *stops.*

GLORIA *takes* MARIA *off stage.*

Oy! There must be an easier way to make a living.

The WEST INDIAN FATHER *comes back on. He finds his family gone.*

Don't worry. They only went for a walk. No luck, my friend?

WEST INDIAN FATHER. 'No colour people.'

SINGER. Psh, prejudice. Racial prejudice.

SINGER *offers his hand to shake. The* WEST INDIAN FATHER *takes it.*

I too have known persecution.

The WEST INDIAN FATHER *nods but is baffled.*

WEST INDIAN FATHER. OK if I use you phone, mister?

He offers money. SINGER *refuses it, and shrugs his assent.*

Look just be quick, don't be in there all day.

WEST INDIAN FATHER. All I'm asking, you know: a roof over my family's head.

SINGER. Of course, of course. There's a housing shortage. It's all these immigrants: Poles, Jews, Irish, Schwarzers. Everybody's got to live somewhere. Someone should do something about it.

The WEST INDIAN FAMILY *troops back on.*

WEST INDIAN FATHER. I even offer to pay extra rent.

SINGER. Of course, of course. My God, it's not as if you're not willing to pay.

WEST INDIAN FATHER. That's right, mister.

SINGER. And pay well, I shouldn't be surprised.

WEST INDIAN FATHER. That's right, mister.

SINGER. Someone could make a fortune.

The WEST INDIAN FATHER *takes his newspaper into the phone box. He's still struggling with the door when* SINGER *has a life-changing idea.*

SINGER. Would one room be enough to sleep in?

WEST INDIAN FATHER. One room is better than no room.

SINGER. Do you say your prayers . . . what's your name?

WEST INDIAN FATHER. Ivanhoe. Yes, sir, I say my prayers.

SINGER. Did you say your prayers this morning, Ivanhoe?

WEST INDIAN FATHER. Yes, sir, I did.

SINGER. Your prayers have been answered. God is looking after you. I have a room empty in my apartment.

MANIK *looks panicky.*

SINGER. Don't worry, Manik, you can sleep with me tonight. Tomorrow we move out and move another family in. Shall we say five pounds a week?

MANIK. Schwarzers!

SINGER. I know they're Schwarzers; this is business!

WEST INDIAN FATHER. Four pounds ten?

SINGER. Two weeks in advance.

The WEST INDIAN FATHER *hands over nine pounds.*

Manik, help the little piccaninnies with their things.

The WEST INDIAN MOTHER *is aghast at the* FATHER. *She's pointing at* SINGER.

WEST INDIAN MOTHER. But, Ivanhoe, he's . . .

WEST INDIAN FATHER. OK. He's Jewish. Do you want to sleep in the park again tonight, girl?

WEST INDIAN MOTHER. But Ivanhoe, he was in the phone box –

WEST INDIAN FATHER. It's his phone box. Come on . . . get along. Things is more sophisticated over here.

They start to troop off towards the apartment.

SINGER. That's it, it's right at the top, offering unrivalled views of Paddington Station. When you enter the spacious hallway, you'll begin to notice already a most unusual aromatic smell.

ACT TWO

Scene One

Enter CHORUS.

CHORUS. How quickly men and women forget. The head men
say we must – or hearts would fill and burst like bladders.
Gone the war, gone the coldest winter of the century – gone
even, nearly gone, memories of crematoria and walking skulls.

It says in the paper the Krauts are getting better off than ever
they were. It says it pays to lose a war, it says, funny idea, and
we're lagging behind; we always were slow starters. The smell,
of course, has gone completely.

He breathes deeply . . .

But now there's a new smell. When I smell I don't smell
decay, I smell . . . change. We've won the war and now we'll
fight the peace.

We're dusting off the covers, things are moving again: that's it:
I can smell *money*. New men are hacking out new fortunes in
the jungle of the City. There are no rules, no rules for
anything now. We used to have Rules of War even, then we
had a war that broke the idea of rules; now we do without –
funny, and that smells fresh as well. There's only one rule
now: big dogs eat little dogs; and Singer – Singer who has no
smell at all, but what a nose for money – has figured out what
people have to have and profits in the wilderness.

In the offices of the MBH Society in London, EX-GROUP CAPTAIN
HARTY, *whose face has been burned off, wears dark glasses and gloves;
with him are* MILLER *and* BLYTHE.

HARTY. Who is this 'Peter Singer'?

MILLER. He started a couple of years ago as a flat-letting agency.
Gradually he's moved into property.

HARTY. Flat letting?

MILLER. Notting Hill – Paddington. A black man in every flat and a white girl in every bed.

HARTY. Then why are we meeting him?

MILLER. He wants to borrow a lot of our money. He says he has a new idea.

BLYTHE. He's got a front the size of Harrods. We met at a drinks party last year. He arrived with a girl not a day over sixteen years old and spent the entire evening trying to persuade my wife to play tennis with him.

MILLER's SECRETARY brings SINGER and MANIK into the outer office.

SINGER is wearing a green suit.

MANIK looks ill.

SINGER. My friend has head problems. Manik, you'd better sit down. Perhaps this gorgeous example of the English rose will fetch you water. Do you like Mozart? I have tickets for a concert tonight. I don't suppose . . .?

She ignores him.

What is it about the English, eh, Manik? The men love money but don't like to be seen making it. With the women it's sex. Can I tell you something? You're sexy.

The SECRETARY hits him in the face just as she shows him into the inner office. SINGER has to stop MANIK from attacking her.

SECRETARY (*introducing him*). Mr Singer, and his personal assistant, Mr Manik.

MILLER. Singer.

SINGER. Mr Miller, Mr Blythe, how are you?

BLYTHE. Have we met? Oh yes. I remember my wife telling me all about you. You certainly amused her.

SINGER. Mrs Blythe . . . fabulous backhand. Didn't she tell you, Vicar? We had a game on grass.

MILLER. This is Ex-Group Captain Harty.

HARTY. Singer.

SINGER. Sir, this is an honour. Captain Harty. My God: I'm talking to a national institution. What courage, what sacrifice.

One of the few. It makes me proud to be British. Not that I
am. They always turn me down. But why *worry*? Here I am
doing business with one of the *few*. *Me*! One of the *many*.

SINGER *laughs too loudly.*

HARTY. You had a quiet war then?

BLYTHE. Not that quiet, I'd've thought.

SINGER. Quiet. Uneventful. My golly. Prosperous even. I was
one of the lucky ones. I got out before it started.

HARTY. Got out of where?

SINGER. Poland.

HARTY. And you, Mr Manik?

MANIK. Germany.

HARTY. Germany?

SINGER. It was all right. He was a communist.

HARTY. A communist.

SINGER. Yes. He suffered in one of the dreadful camps. You
know what he says when he's feeling funny? 'I ate shit, but I
never ate German shit!' Isn't that a hoot? They hit him on the
head a lot, now he gets headaches. Manik, Captain Harty got
all his face burned off in a Spitfire in the war. He's a hero.
Look at those scars.

HARTY. I'd rather he didn't, if you don't mind.

SINGER. Don't be a silly goose, it's good for us to meet heroes.
Manik, go and sit down. Did you give him that water, dear?

MANIK *goes back out to the* SECRETARY.

SINGER *has alienated all three of them.*

Well? Shall we talk business?

MILLER. I think it's pretty unlikely that our interests will be
mutual given the scale of your business and its particular
flavour.

SINGER. Particular flavour? Oh you mean 'schwarz und tarts'?
Now let me see if I understand the particular flavour of the
MBH Property Group. Miller, Blythe, Harty Property Group.

First of all you need property to buy, preferably at knock-down prices; that's where the vicar comes into it.

BLYTHE. I'm not a bloody vicar, I'm a solicitor.

SINGER. Of course you are, Mr Blythe, but you represent the property interests of the Church Commissioners – so that sort of makes you holy, doesn't it? The Church Commissioners own run-down property – big estates – all over London, yeah, it's embarrassing – they're overcrowded slums – they want to sell them off. And you sold a lot of them – to MBH Property Group.

BLYTHE. So?

SINGER. So nothing. Business is business. God knows. But what good is cheap property without cheap money to buy it? No problem. Mr Miller starts the Miller Building Society and people fall over themselves to lend him their savings at very low rates and he uses it to give cheap mortgages to the MBH Property Group. But why, I hear Mr Manik asking himself, would people trust such a new building society? That's where the Group Captain comes into it. As well as being a paid director of the MBH Property Group, Captain Harty also decorates the board of the Miller Building Society for a modest salary, in return for which you give the investor the assurance he needs that his money is in safe hands. Because they would worry, wouldn't they, Captain, if they thought their money was in the hands of crooks?

There is a silence.

MILLER. You mentioned some 'idea'.

SINGER. Yes. It's a good idea – all I need is access to cheap money. I'm applying for a mortgage. Or two.

SINGER *takes out the details of a house and shows them it.*

BLYTHE. You want to buy a house?

SINGER. I've bought it. On bridging finance. 12 per cent. Aye, aye, aye. I'd like to start a bank, wouldn't you, Mr Miller?

MILLER. You want to mortgage it with us?

SINGER. That's all, old boys.

MILLER. Why didn't you just ask? There was no need –

SINGER. Because this house in Shepherds Bush cost me £4,000. I'd like to mortgage it with you for £10,000.

MILLER. I can't do that. Anything over £5,000 has to be shown in our annual return. We can't get away with things like that.

SINGER. But I told you I have an idea.

1. I buy a house for £4,000.

2. I split it into five apartments.

3. You give me five mortgages of £2,000 each.

4. I let the five flats out at a total rental of £1,000 per annum.

5. The rent pays the five mortgage repayments.

6. I keep the difference of £6,000.

7. I do it again.

8. I do it again.

9. I do it again.

He takes out a huge portfolio of properties he wishes to buy on mortgage.

And again. And again. And again. And again. Until I am a very rich man.

They are taking it in.

Why don't you take a moment to think about it, gentlemen?

SINGER *is by now sitting in* MILLER's *chair.*

You will need to talk. Why not use the outer office?

They go off stage with the portfolio of properties.

SINGER *lights one of* MILLER's *cigars.*

MANIK *comes in and sits. He lights one of* MILLER's *cigars too.*

Outside daylight is fading.

MANIK. OK, Boss?

SINGER. OK, Manik. How's the head?

MANIK. OK, now. Now it has tickety-boo. Hey, Uncle Peter, this old boy with half his face burned off. We shouldn't be picking on him.

SINGER. Manik. Do you remember the day we arrived in

England? You, me and Stefan, we all lined up and we said goodbye to Stefan – God, are you listening, I'd give ten years off my life to see Stefan again – and we all got onto buses.

The SECRETARY *comes in and stands listening.*

MANIK. I cried all the way, Uncle Peter.

SINGER. Of course you did. I told you we were going to California.

MANIK. Why didn't we go to California?

SINGER. They wouldn't have us. It was England or Israel. Can you imagine us picking oranges on a kibbutz? Life's too short. Well anyway, comrade, you remember we had to walk the last ten miles to Slough.

MANIK. I wanted to die.

SINGER. We all wanted to die when we saw Slough.

MANIK. This is why we are picking on the Captain?

SINGER. The reason we had to walk was no petrol. Remember petrol rationing? People would do anything to get extra petrol. People syphoned petrol from cars parked in the street. Sometimes a nasty accident occurred, a spark, a careless match, and whoosh! A fellow could lose half his face. The nearest the Captain got to Spitfires was when his lips were burning.

MANIK. Oh! Whoosh!

SECRETARY. What's all this about Mozart then? I don't know nothing about classical music, I'm warning you.

SINGER. I'll teach you. Before the war I was a concert pianist.

SECRETARY. Where was that?

SINGER. What does it matter, comrade? It doesn't exist anymore.

MILLER, HARTY *and* BLYTHE *come back.*

BLYTHE. There's nothing illegal about what you're asking.

SINGER. I didn't say there was. Not everybody's crooked, Your Holiness.

MILLER. Just very risky.

SINGER. I'm asking you to take a risk. My dear, this gentleman will escort you to my waiting car.

BLYTHE. You know, every single one of these properties has a sitting tenant.

SINGER. Yeah.

MILLER. Your scheme can only work if you evict these people.

SINGER. Yeah.

HARTY. And they're usually very old people.

SINGER. Yeah –

BLYTHE. How are you going to get them out?

SINGER smiles and leaves.

Scene Two

A street in Shepherds Bush. Night. A sturdy front house-door with a window light above it.

Enter SINGER, *who carries a bucket of pennies, and* MANIK, *who wheels a wheelbarrow.*

SINGER. Remember, Manik, keep out of sight till I give the signal.

MANIK. But, Uncle Peter –

SINGER. Screw your courage to the sticky point.

SINGER makes sure MANIK is invisible from the doorway, takes the bucket in one hand and raps on the door.

A dog barks fiercely inside.

A light comes on above the door. A WOMAN'*s voice is heard.*

MRS DALEY. Who is it?

SINGER. Nobody at all, dear Mrs Daley. Only I, Mr Singer, the owner of the property.

Her head appears in the window above the door. She scrutinises him.

SINGER smiles ingratiatingly.

MRS DALEY. Go away.

SINGER. My dear, charming lady. I have to empty the gas meter. This I am obliged to do by law.

SINGER *jingles the coins in the bucket.*

MRS DALEY. Piss off!

SINGER. Then I'm afraid I just have to come in. I'm coming in now, Mrs Daley. Here I come.

He tries to turn the lock. The key doesn't fit.

It was very naughty, naughty of you to change the lock. Look. Here is a very official letter from the magistrates ordering me to empty the meter. I'm posting it now. Here it comes.

SINGER *posts the letter through the letterbox. He gets his hand bitten.*

The letter comes back through the box, in shreds.

MRS DALEY. An Englishman's home is his castle.

SINGER. But you're Irish.

An old MAN's *head now appears.*

MR DALEY. You keep a civil tongue in your head!

SINGER. Aye, aye, now Mr Punch arrives. Get ready.

MANIK *prepares himself with gloves and a length of cord.*

MR DALEY. Who're you talking to?

SINGER. Only to myself, who else? My dear sir, you know it is forbidden to keep a dog in my house.

MR DALEY. Clear off. He's trained to bite Jews.

SINGER *opens the letterbox.*

SINGER. But can't he see I'm Polish? (*In Polish.*) My dear, sweet little doggy, I'm Polish.

The dog has another go at him.

Dear people, what we are talking about here is The March of Progress. You are living – to put it bluntly, like pigs in shit.

MRS DALEY. You turned the water off, that's why.

SINGER. Let's face facts. You're not getting any younger. Let me take you away from all this. A cosy retirement home is yours for the asking – get ready, Manik – and here, without prejudice, is a gift of £50 to set you on your way – be ruthless with them once you're in – from me to you, out of deep respect for your advancing years. And in order to avoid the situation escalating into a ruinously expensive court case for you, or even *violence*. Which I abhor. Manik. How about it?

He waves the banknotes in the air.

MR DALEY. Piss off.

SINGER. Then you leave me no choice, I'll have to call the police.

The OLD PAIR *confer.*

MR DALEY. The police. We'll have to let him in.

MRS DALEY. He's not coming in.

MR DALEY. He has to come in, it's the law.

MRS DALEY. He's not coming in.

MR DALEY. You have to let him in.

MRS DALEY. I won't have him in.

MR DALEY. Do as you're bloody told.

SINGER. That's the way to do it.

Silence. The heads have disappeared. The door opens, slowly. The dog growls menacingly.

SINGER *signals to* MANIK *who dashes in. The door slams shut. Terrible cries of man and animal.*

SINGER *stands listening.*

MANIK. Hau ab-Du verflüchter dummer Hund. Ich dreh Dir Deinen bloden Hals um. Du glaubst Du Kannst mir angst einjagen-dummes Misvich verreck Du gemeines Tier.

Eventually we hear the OLD PAIR *screaming as* MANIK *strangles the dog. The door flies open and* MANIK, *his face gashed, his mouth bloody, drags the* OLD PAIR *on to the street.*

MANIK. Raus, raus.

MR DALEY. This animal bit our dog.

MANIK. Der shitty Hund bit me first, Uncle Peter.

MANIK *goes back in.*

MRS DALEY. What right have you to do this?

SINGER. It's my house. That's what rights I've got. If you want rights, buy some property.

MANIK *drags out the dead dog by the cord around its neck.*

MR DALEY. Rebel! Rebel, are you dead?

MRS DALEY. We've had him since a pup!

SINGER. Please calm yourselves.

SINGER *hands them some pennies.*

Here, buy yourselves another doggie.

The OLD PEOPLE *are wailing.*

MANIK *is dragging their belongings out and dumping them in the street.*

A POLICE CONSTABLE *comes on.*

MR DALEY. Officer, Officer.

MRS DALEY. Please, please, help us. He's the landlord. He's throwing us out into the streets.

PC. Is this true, sir?

SINGER. Yes Officer, it's true. I *am* the landlord.

PC (*to the* OLD PAIR). Shut up!

Stunned, the OLD PAIR *shut up.*

SINGER. Thank you, Officer.

PC. That's all right, sir.

The POLICE CONSTABLE *strolls off.*

MANIK *comes out and locks up with their keys. The* OLD MAN *carries the dog. The* WOMAN *pushes the barrow.*

MRS DALEY. I'll be revenged. Rebel's spirit will never die.

THEY *go off.*

MANIK *gives the keys to* SINGER. *He is looking remorseful.*

SINGER. What are you sniffling for?

MANIK. Uncle. I am thinking Uncle. My mother. She too was forced out of her home. I am thinking.

SINGER. Don't *think* Manik. It's suicidal for you. You can remember a mother?

MANIK *cries.*

MANIK. Sometimes.

SINGER. What can you remember, Manik? It's important. What was her name?

MANIK. No name. But a face. Such a lovely face. I cannot tell you.

SINGER. Beautiful face, I'm sure. I can picture her. I had a mother too.

SINGER *is weeping now as well.*

TWIN *girls, aged about 20, walk on and linger nearby.*

MANIK. Soft skin.

SINGER. Clear, white skin. No. Don't think.

SINGER *catches sight of the twin girls.*

MANIK. And, do you know Uncle Peter? When she spoke to us children her voice was so gentle, and so . . .

SINGER. Manik what about those tits! Four of them! Aren't they beautiful. Do you think they're on the game?

MANIK. But Uncle –

SINGER. Manik don't *worry*. Nothing *matters*. Look at those buttocks – like two pairs of serving bowls.

MANIK. Uncle Peter, what I am saying: does nothing matter? The old woman –

But SINGER *has already left him.*

SINGER. Excuse me, young ladies, can I be of assistance, however small or large?

MANIK. We can't get away with throwing old ladies on to the streets, just because . . . just because.

SINGER. Can't we?

MANIK. Nothing matters?

SINGER. So why worry?

SINGER *stoops and pretends to find a wad of notes on the ground. Really they were in his hand.*

My goodness, there must be £50 here! Girls have you checked your purses?

The GIRLS *check their bags as* SINGER *goes to them.*

MANIK. Maybe I should leave and get an honest job like what maybe I had before. All Peter can tell me: my hands were soft when first he knows me. So not a hard job. Teacher maybe. All I know: I was a whole man. I was a whole man who wanted his life and no headaches.

SINGER *now has a* GIRL *on each arm.*

MANIK. Two girls tonight. No sleep for Uncle Peter. Is good. No need for Manik to sit and talk tonight. To keep the dreams away. Many nights I listen. 'Manik,' he says, 'there's nobody left. From all the houses and the streets where we live. All dead. Except two. Peter Singer, who cannot sleep. And Stefan Gutman, who went in Kirkcudbright so he would never forget Lvov.'

SINGER. Manik, don't forget that bucket full of pennies.

SINGER *and the* TWINS *go.*

MANIK *stays.*

MANIK. I found Stefan. He lives beside the railway at Clapham and makes photographs for his living. Peter must meet Stefan. It was a joy to see him after so many years, but he has heard of Uncle Peter and how he makes his money – even in Clapham he has heard – he says the Peter Singer he knew died in Poland. Only my head was cracked, Peter's heart is split open.

MANIK *leaves, carrying the bucket full of pennies.*

Enter SHALLCROSS, PEPPER, SCHOFIELD, *a press photographer, and* ANOTHER.

PEPPER. Get after the old pair with the barrow. Get good pictures. I want real tears mind.

SHALLCROSS. Only pay if absolutely necessary.

SCHOFIELD *makes to go.*

Oi! Schofield.

SCHOFIELD *pauses for more instructions.*

Don't forget the dog. And meet us in The Flask in Hampstead before drinking-up time.

SCHOFIELD *goes.*

PEPPER. Twins! – He loves anything over the top. He's in the grip of excess, Shallcross. Get shots of wherever he puts his hands!

SHALLCROSS. But don't let him see you!

The SECOND PHOTOGRAPHER *goes.*

PEPPER. What do you smell?

SHALLCROSS. A good story, Pepper, an exposé.

PEPPER. 'From out of the camps he came, a man out of –'

SHALLCROSS. 'Creature'.

PEPPER. 'A creature every shred of human feeling out of whom had been beaten. In Germany he survived a concentration camp, in England he built an empire of slums.'

SHALLCROSS. 'With his vicious side-kick, half animal, half man – he terrorised defenceless people showing no pity when they begged for mercy.'

PEPPER. And photos: photos of the old pair sleeping on the streets, photos of Singer mixing with the upper crust, gate crashing where he's not welcome; playing *chemin de fer* and blackjack with people up whose shoelaces he's not worthy of doing.

SHALLCROSS. Got it: banner headline over a picture of him groping the twins. 'GET YOUR DIRTY FOREIGN HANDS OFF OUR WOMEN!'

PEPPER. No. 'Foreign Landlord With Taste for Vice Girls' . . . No.

SHALLCROSS. No. 'Foreign Vice Landlord' –

PEPPER. Racketeer! 'Foreign Slum Vice Landlord Racketeer'! . . .

SHALLCROSS. No. 'Concentration Camp Slum Landlord Racketeer Pictured In Upper-Class Drug Addict Vice Ring Hideaway.' 'Near Palace.'

PEPPER. No, no, no. It lacks pith. Back to basics. Religion.

SHALLCROSS. Jewish.

PEPPER. Social Conscience.

SHALLCROSS. Slum.

PEPPER. Royalty.

SHALLCROSS. King.

PEPPER. Sport.

SHALLCROSS. Ladies' Doubles.

PEPPER. Sex.

SHALLCROSS. Romp. 'Jewish Slum King In Ladies' Doubles Sex Romp.'

They cheer.

BOTH. We name the guilty man!

They both exit.

ACT THREE

Scene One

A painting and photographic studio in a house near Clapham Junction. There are lights and tripods. There are canvasses and paints.

Enter CHORUS, *dressed for a photo session.*

CHORUS. Listen! Can you hear them? There are words again. Not clapped-out old words stunned out of their senses by the size of the problem, but baby words with innocent meanings. Not words that drive men inwards and downwards to worlds best forgotten – but words that fly like larks to the heart of things that matter most. Television set. Deodorant. Twin tub. Ready-to-bake. Refrigerator. Now the never-never takes the waiting out of wanting and nothing is that cannot be bought, nothing is wished that cannot be fulfilled; no desire that cannot be created, and in that brief painful moment of its birth when you realise you must have it but you don't know what it *is*, be immediately priced and gift-wrapped. No. There's no pain, no longing for that unidentified something-missing-in-my life – for every stabbing need can have a local anaesthetic and a name. Or, as someone put it better in words of one syllable: most of you have never had it so good. 'Most'? There's a mean word: a word to spoil a party. Not 'all' then? One New Elizabethan at least – a stranger on the shore perhaps – not able to get his nose in the trough? Not able – or not willing? Does London harbour such a freak? O, consumer unendurable. Where is he who won't boom with us while the band plays? Well then: picture if you will a place where everybody changes but one man stays the same. At the Junction, where trains come and go every sixty seconds, one man never moves. For here – in Clapham – something extraordinary is taking place. Here in Clapham – where that statistically ordinary man sits forever on that proverbially ordinary omnibus waiting to be asked his quintessentially ordinary opinions – here, at the hub of everydayness, something like a miracle has happened. While everybody around him grew older, Stefan stayed the same. As if to remind him of the childish faces he once counted, his own won't add a single day. While London bristles with Angry Young Men, in its still centre sits an Old Boy who hasn't turned a hair.

CHORUS *takes his place in front of the camera.*

STEFAN *turns on the lights.*

STEFAN. Say 'cheese'.

CHORUS. Hard lines.

(*He pays* STEFAN *and goes.*)

STEFAN (*singing in Polish*). Potatoes on Sunday, potatoes on Monday, potatoes on Tuesday.

SINGER (*hidden*). Potatoes on Wednesday.

STEFAN *listens, looks around. Nothing. He decides to clear up. He pushes away the backdrop. Behind it is a giant seaside scene with holes for people's heads to poke through.* SINGER's *head is visible above a skinny body in a striped bathing costume.* STEFAN *doesn't see it at first – then he sees* SINGER. *He is silent.*

STEFAN. Who are you, please?

SINGER *comes out and stands in front of him. He's wearing a hat and dark glasses.*

SINGER. He doesn't see me. That's good. Manik was right. Stefan hasn't changed.

A man who would like his portrait.

STEFAN. Ah.

SINGER. A photograph. A snapshot that is.

STEFAN. Ah. Good. Please sit down.

He sits SINGER *in a chair and chooses a background.*

Anything in particular?

SINGER. Something dignified. It's for my passport. I'm going to be British.

STEFAN. Ah. I too am British.

SINGER. You are?

STEFAN. Three years.

SINGER. They gave you a passport three years ago?

STEFAN. Yes. They kept giving me a form so eventually I filled it in. It makes life easier. Sit still please.

He arranges the lights.

A train passes by.

SINGER. Don't the trains trouble you?

STEFAN. Yes, in some ways they do. In other ways it's good to hear the sound of trains.

SINGER. I can't help noticing your tattoo. Don't you keep it hidden? Now you are British.

STEFAN. Why should I hide it? To your right.

SINGER. Some people do.

STEFAN. I have nothing to be ashamed of.

SINGER. But some people say, you know, 'You're showing this in order to get special treatment'.

STEFAN (*chuckling*). It was Special Treatment that got me this. I'm not asking for any more, believe me.

SINGER. You can laugh about it then?

STEFAN. Can you take off your hat and glasses, please?

SINGER. I'm told you are a painter. As well as taking snaps. You splash paint around as well. Well?

STEFAN. Well what?

SINGER. Is this true?

STEFAN. I paint sometimes.

SINGER. English landscapes?

STEFAN. No.

SINGER. What – no English landscapes? What about scenes of English life? The Changing of the Guard. The Lord Mayor's Show. The Notting Hill Race Riot.

STEFAN. No. Only Polish subjects. The hat and glasses, please.

SINGER. Polish? Why Polish? If you're so proud of this British

passport you never stop blowing your trumpet over, why not
have the decency to paint the Epsom Derby or Robin Hood
and his Merry Men? He robbed the rich to help the poor,
what a schlemiel! He wants to be the Chancellor of the
Exchequer. Well?

STEFAN. It's really quite simple. I still think and feel in Polish.
And this – these things I paint are very personal.

SINGER. Personal? Such as what? Personal experiences?

STEFAN. Yes.

SINGER. Like what?

STEFAN. There are certain things it is very important to try to
make sense with. Things that were not without significance.
Hold still now.

STEFAN *looks into the image finder.*

SINGER *removes his hat and glasses and at last* STEFAN *sees him.*

STEFAN *remains looking a long time.*

SINGER *nods.*

SINGER. And have you made any sense at all with it, Stefan?

They kiss and hug and cry and call out each other's names in Polish.

Manik told me all about you. I've been at the door three times
and not been able to cross it. He says you didn't want to see
me.

STEFAN. Manik is getting fat. It's good.

SINGER. He's with me – and Stefan: I'm rich.

STEFAN. Yes, I heard you were rich.

SINGER. Listen, there's room for you. I have a new house the
size of a football stadium. You can work for me. You don't
have to do any more painting or take snaps.

STEFAN. Not do painting?

SINGER. That's all in the past – people don't want to be
reminded.

STEFAN. But I want to remind them. It had a cause and a
meaning.

SINGER. But don't you understand what I'm saying? I'm *rich*. I'm shitting fivers. If you want to paint, come and paint Peter Singer in his new house.

STEFAN (*after a pause*). Yes, OK – of course.

SINGER. The room I work in burns with gold leaf. The desk is solid walnut inlaid with turquoise. The bed I sleep in came from Versailles. You know how much it cost me?

STEFAN. How much?

SINGER. Don't ask. There's plenty more where that came from.

STEFAN. Where *did* it come from?

SINGER. Believe me, in this country there is nothing you cannot do, nobody you cannot have. Look at me, a penniless nobody when I arrived, and now, though I say so myself, a man . . . Well . . . A man who . . . Well. I am a man. I am a man.

There is a pause.

STEFAN *smiles.*

STEFAN. Not just any man. A *British* man.

SINGER. Yes. In time. These things take time.

STEFAN. Oh. But I thought . . .

SINGER. Stefan. I'm as good as any of them.

STEFAN. Better.

SINGER. Better. Did I tell you about the dining-room? The ceiling will pull your eyes out. Will you come?

STEFAN. Like a shot.

SINGER. Good. Thank you. Bring a bag. Stay a while.

STEFAN. No wife, Peter?

SINGER. Well, you know me: I like girls, young girls. If I married one of them she'd grow old. Like I'm doing. Are you alone? You must have many friends. Artists, maybe.

There is a pause.

STEFAN *shrugs.*

Look, I've got an idea. This house is ridiculously large – of course I do a lot of entertaining. I have many, many friends and business associates and valued colleagues in the property world – why not have a room there, or two or three?

STEFAN. My life is here. But I'll come to visit.

SINGER. Yes.

SINGER*'s happy about this at least. He's reluctant to leave though.*

Are you alone? You didn't say how many friends.

STEFAN. You remember the old saying in Lvov: If you say you have one true friend, you're well off; if you say you have two good friends, you're a lucky man; if you say you have three good friends, you're a liar.

SINGER. Ah, that was Lvov. Lvov was a small place really. Those people are all dead. Well . . . I've got so much to do old friend . . .

SINGER. Stefcho.

STEFAN. Yes?

SINGER. Do you sleep?

STEFAN. Yes, Uncle Peter, I sleep.

MANIK *rushes in clutching a letter.*

MANIK. Uncle Peter, Uncle Peter!

MANIK *hugs* STEFAN.

Stefan. Cor blimey. Uncle Peter. A letter has come.

SINGER. Manik, what is it, your Premium Bond has come up? Her Majesty has invited you to Balmoral for Christmas?

MANIK. For you. 'Home Office.'

MANIK *hands the letter over.*

SINGER *rips it open and reads.*

Silence.

He cries.

STEFAN. What is it, Peter?

SINGER. I'm British. I'm British! I'm not a stateless person anymore! I have a home!

STEFAN. Congratulations!

MANIK. Top hole, Uncle Peter!

SINGER. I'm going to throw a party as big as Selfridges! Let's get going. The cream of Society will be invited – Stefan! You will be the guest of honour!

STEFAN (*pleased*). OK.

SINGER. Just wait and see, Stefan. You thought Lvov was sophisticated. Forget it: wait till you see the cream of London Society at my house! Lvov was just East Grinstead!

SINGER *goes*.

MANIK (*vocalises*). Peter, he's different now.

STEFAN. Yes. In some ways.

MANIK. He wants we should be all together. In Hampstead. In the big house like a football stadium.

STEFAN. I will stay here.

MANIK. Is best to come, Stefan.

STEFAN. You can come here anytime, Manik. It will be good to have friends again. Would you like a picture of you? Photograph. Free of charge.

MANIK. For who? What I want, you cannot give. A picture of Manik before. Remember what I was before. Maybe you have a magic camera, yah? (*He laughs.*) That I would put in my pocket. Just to have. Yah.

STEFAN *seems uneasy about this idea*.

You come to Hampstead. Is best for you.

STEFAN. It's OK for me here. I live cheap. Church of England is my landlord. It's not a good house but my rent is twenty-three shillings only.

MANIK. You have new landlord now. From three days. Whole block. Whole block.

STEFAN *lets this sink in*.

There will be changes, Stefan. It is the March of Progress.

STEFAN. Did he know it was my home?

MANIK *won't look at him*.

Don't worry, Manik. I know Peter. He would never do that to me.

MANIK *looks at him. He doesn't agree.*

MANIK. Peter, he's different now. Cor blimey. I got to go. Don't tell Peter anything I tell you. He blow his top at me again. I get another headache then.

MANIK *chuckles. He stops. He starts to go.*

STEFAN. Manik.

MANIK *stops.*

STEFAN *moves all the screens away. He leads* MANIK *to the curtain and draws it back to reveal a half-completed giant mural showing children's faces as they run naked into the gas blocks. Singer with his bowl of soup. Stefan's haunted face watching the children. Manik as he was before he was beaten.*

MANIK *stares at himself. He touches his image.* MANIK *closes the curtain and walks out slowly.*

The lights begin to flicker.

STEFAN *looks up. The lights go out.*

Scene Two

A room in SINGER's *palatial Hampstead home.* MANIK *sits to one side, alone, in evening dress, uncomfortable.*

SERVANTS *carry on tables groaning with food and wine.*

MUSICIANS *tune up. This is all done as quietly as is physically possible.*

A SERVANT *clinks two wine glasses together by accident.* EVERYONE *freezes. They listen. Nothing. They carry on.*

MANIK *takes his hand out of his pocket and looks at it. He sings quietly to himself.*

MANIK (*singing*). My left hand has five fingers
    Five fingers has my hand
    If it did not have five fingers
    It would not be my hand.

My other hand has five fingers
Five fingers has my hand.

MANIK realises all the SERVANTS *are staring at him. He puts his hand back in his pocket.*

They carry on preparing for the party. Someone drops a spoon into a bowl. There is an immediate cry offstage.

SINGER (*offstage*). Aaaagh!

SINGER enters.

How can I sleep with all this noise all the time?!

SINGER looks haggard.

The SERVANTS *are all terrified of him.*

Who is responsible?

BUTLER. It was the new girl, sir.

SINGER. She's dismissed.

The BUTLER *snaps his fingers and the* GIRL *leaves.*

Who are these people?

BUTLER. Musicians, sir.

SINGER. Why aren't they playing? Am I paying them a fee to sit around with their fingers up their arse?

BUTLER. No sir, of course not.

The BUTLER *signals the* MUSICIANS *to play. They do so quietly.*

SINGER. Carry on.

SINGER watches them carry on preparing for the party.

Manik. Come, come. Was it carried out? Did you go to Clapham and see for yourself?

MANIK. Yes, but – Uncle Peter –

SINGER. Yes or no?

MANIK. Yes.

SINGER. Good. How long did I sleep?

MANIK. Forty-two minutes you were asleep, Uncle. Not bad.

SINGER. I dreamt.

MANIK. Uncle Peter, about Stefan, there comes a time when even I have to say –

But a SERVANT *passes by carrying a stack of plates to the table and* SINGER *follows like a dog following a scent; ignoring* MANIK. SINGER *examines the stack of plates until, halfway down he discovers a speck of dirt.*

SINGER. Aaiee! Who is responsible? What is this? What is it? That.

SINGER *points to the speck of dirt.*

The SERVANTS *gather round and look, but fail to see it.*

That! There! There!

SERVANT. It's part of the pattern.

SINGER. It's not the pattern. It's filthy shit! Are you trying to get me to eat shit? Throw it away.

SERVANT. But, Mr Singer, it only needs a wash.

SINGER. Don't wash it. Throw it away.

SERVANT. But, Mr Singer, this is –

SINGER *takes the plate, smashes it over the* SERVANT*'s head and hands him the pieces.*

SINGER. Throw it away. He's dismissed.

The SERVANT *goes.*

SINGER *turns on the other* SERVANTS.

Well? There are guests arriving any minute. Get my clothes ready. Run me a bath.

The SERVANTS *depart.*

SINGER *begins examining plates and cutlery.*

MANIK. Uncle Peter – There comes a time –

SINGER. Manik, get to the door, will you? I want you to deal ruthlessly with gatecrashers. Nobody to be admitted without one of these!

SINGER *waves the printed invitation.*

Did Stefan get his?

MANIK. I gave it to him myself.

SINGER. Will he come?

MANIK. Yes, he comes, but Uncle –

SINGER (*reading from the card*). A party to celebrate the granting of British Citizenship to Peter Singer Esquire. Evening dress to be worn.

A SERVANT *enters.*

SERVANT. Your bath's waiting, Mr Singer.

SINGER. OK.

MANIK *stands looking glumly at the invitations.*

MANIK. Uncle Peter, I don't want to be letting you down, Uncle. It's a big problem. Cor blimey.

SINGER. Manik, for God's sake, I'm busy. Sort it out yourself, can't you? 'Cor blimey' already!

MANIK. But, Uncle – what I'm saying is –

SINGER. Look, no more of this 'Uncle Peter' this and 'Uncle Peter' that, OK? It makes my colleagues laugh. Even the other servants laugh at you.

MANIK. 'Other servants'?

SINGER. You are fifty years old for God's sake and frankly a bloody liability. OK, I give you a job because nobody else can be expected to employ such a baby brain but it was never my intention it should go on forever – I'm not responsible for you till the day you fall off your perch, am I?

There is a silence.

MANIK *doesn't know what to say.*

SINGER *relents.*

Manik . . . this is a big occasion for me. These are the cream coming here tonight. At last I'm not just some nobody. I'm British. These people respect me. I make them money. You see, Manik, I'm surprised I have to tell you this but it's something you obviously haven't noticed: I've become a very important man.

MANIK. Sorry, Unc . . . Mr Singer.

SINGER. That's OK. What is it?

MANIK. People have much questions.

The doorbell rings.

MANIK *holds his head.*

SINGER *touches him fondly.*

There is trouble.

SINGER. OK, you've got a problem. Somebody won't pay his rent. Somebody's complaining about blocked drains. Always complaints.

MANIK. No, no.

Again MANIK *puts his head in his hands.*

SINGER. It makes your head hurt. But do me a favour, not tonight: take some of your pills and bring me the problem tomorrow – Yah?

MANIK *nods.*

Now go to the door, please. And remember: if they show no invitation, you show no mercy. Out on their arses.

SINGER *goes.*

Guests start coming in. MANIK *grabs invitations and scrutinises them and their bearers. He is treated like a dangerous animal.*

BUTLER. Group Captain Harty. Lord and Lady Bunty. Sir Basil and Lady Basil. Mr Stefan Gutman.

The GUESTS *are given drinks and stare about the room in disbelief.*

The music stops.

LORD EARNER. Have you ever seen anything quite so ghastly? Is this a zebra skin we are standing on?

LADY BUNTY. Where is our host?

SIR BASIL. Upstairs with a couple of fillies I expect.

There is laughter.

Wouldn't mind joining him.

More laughter.

LADY BASIL. That'll be the day.

LORD EARNER. Not that sort of party, is it, Basil?

LORD BUNTY. You can never tell with Singer.

More laughter.

SIR BASIL (*To* STEFAN). Get me a scotch, would you?

STEFAN *does so.*

LORD BUNTY. Some pretty peculiar people here as well.

They look at STEFAN *and his clothes as he brings the scotch.*

LADY BUNTY. He's the guest of honour, Eric.

LORD EARNER. Look, I suggest we try and keep this as brief as
we decently can, then bugger off about 9.30. I know where
there's a roulette wheel if anyone's interested.

There is enthusiasm.

STEFAN (*too loudly*). No, you mustn't do that!

They gape at him.

LORD BUNTY. You and Singer go back a long way Mr . . .?

STEFAN. Gutman. Yes, we had a saying: To know a man you
must ride in the same wagon as him.

LADY BUNTY. Ah.

LADY BASIL. Charming proverb.

STEFAN. Not a proverb but a fact.

LADY BUNTY. What wagon was that?

STEFAN. The wagon to Auschwitz. Here's your Scotch.

He gives the Scotch to SIR BASIL.

LADY BUNTY. One question always comes back to me. If there
were really six million of you, why didn't you resist?

STEFAN. Some did. As for the rest, should Hiroshima have
resisted its atom bomb?

STEFAN *could kick himself.*

A fanfare.

Enter SINGER, *overdressed.*

SINGER. Harty. Basil. Lady Basil, Lord Bunty, Lady Bunty. Lord
Earner, how are you?

LORD EARNER. Well, thank you, Singer.

SINGER. And how is Lady Earner and all those nice little Earners?

LORD EARNER. Sends her apologies. In bed with a headache.

SINGER. In bed with who?

LORD EARNER. A headache.

Laughter.

LADY BUNTY. You're terrible, Peter.

SINGER. I am, aren't I?

LORD EARNER. Oh, before I forget, she says she'd like another game of tennis sometime.

SINGER. She must be desperate.

LORD EARNER. Yes, I think she is.

SINGER. Yes, I think she is.

LORD EARNER. She keeps saying her service is useless.

SINGER. Has she tried refrigerating the balls? (*He laughs.*)

LORD EARNER. Ladies present, Singer.

SINGER. Eat, eat.

There is embarrassment. They go into a huddle at the food table.

SINGER *sees* STEFAN *and greets him warmly, though he can't help noticing he isn't dressed correctly.*

SINGER. Stefan. Well. What do you think?

STEFAN. It's quite impressive.

SINGER. Not just the house. What about the guests? Stefan, you should be clever and circulate. You could get commissions. You could be painting their daughters on their ponies.

STEFAN. Who are they, Peter?

SINGER. These people are my livelihood and I am theirs. I buy their old property – old houses that have been in the family for years – they're too lazy to make them pay, *I* make them pay. Some of them are men I borrow money from to buy the houses. Naturally they lend me money at very advantageous

rates – advantageous to them. 25 per cent. But why worry?
You just keep moving it around, buy more properties, raise
more and more mortgages to pay off the old ones. And you
can never stop. It's a very merry-go-round. All morning I do
this. And in the afternoons I screw their wives which they also
cannot be bothered to do. I borrow their money and I borrow
their wives. So you see, Stefan, none of it is mine.

SINGER *laughs.*

STEFAN *doesn't.*

So you're not enjoying yourself, obviously.

STEFAN. Something strange has happened. Last week my
electricity supply was cut off. So what? I live in the dark, I've
had a lot worse. This week men came with hacksaws and
removed sections from all the water pipes. I had to work hard
to save my paintings from water damage.

SINGER. Psssh. There are some bastards in the world. Have you
told the police? The police here are very good. Manik, don't
stand gawping. You saved your paintings then? You'll have to
show me them some day.

STEFAN. It was the landlord, I'm sure.

SINGER. Oh no, I wouldn't think so . . .

STEFAN. Why are you doing this to me?

SINGER. What?

STEFAN. What right do you think you have?

SINGER. I don't know what you mean. Look, no problem, you
can live here. All problems solved. It's quiet here. You can
work, even paint, live as you please: I'll build your own front
door for you round the back.

STEFAN. Why are you persecuting me?

SINGER. Stefan . . .

SINGER *tries to laugh it off. He's unaware they are becoming the focus
of attention.*

STEFAN. It's true what they say about you, isn't it? Well, isn't it?
Perhaps you can't forgive me because I remind you of what we
really are!

SINGER. We shouldn't be living in slums like that! For God's sake, what are you proving? What does it prove? Any bastard can live in a slum. Blacks, Irish, all live in poverty and dirt!

MANIK *is distressed at the developing row.*

STEFAN. You should know.

SINGER. Yes I should know. What does it prove – that you're superior? Because you live in a hovel – without even basic amenities like water and light, that's something to be proud of – and dress like a refugee from a soup kitchen? How dare you come here to my house dressed like that?!

MANIK. Please, Mr Singer, your guests –

STEFAN. 'Mr Singer'?

SINGER. What the hell are you doing here? You should be on the door.

LORD EARNER *is tapping his glass but* SINGER *doesn't notice.*

Who knows what bloody riff-raff might be in here. You can throw this one out for a start.

Silence. He sees everyone looking at him. He smiles winningly.

STEFAN (*in Polish*). With all my heart. (*He unwraps a gift and puts it in* SINGER's *hand. It's a bowl from the camp.*)

LORD EARNER. Well, let's have a toast then, shall we?

BUTLER. Charge your glasses, ladies and gentlemen.

ALL. Toast, toast.

SINGER's *bowl is filled with champagne.*

LORD EARNER. To Peter Singer, now truly and belatedly and thoroughly deservedly one of us.

There is applause.

ALL. One of us. (*They toast him*). Speech. Speech.

SINGER *dabs tears from his eyes.*

SINGER. Thank you. You cannot know what this means to me: a man who was robbed of everything to stand here now in this beautiful house which is mortgaged to the hilt with you Sir Basil and – yes, I can say it – among friends. It is an achievement I should take deep pleasure from: British at last. And yet as I stand here, an immigrant from foreign soil, a mere sapling in the shadow of these mighty oaks who reach down into the deepest roots of British society, I realise that I stand only in the foothills of achievement. For Lord Earner, your grandfather too was an immigrant – in your case a poor starving refugee from famine-torn Ireland.

LORD EARNER *looks a little embarrassed at this revelation.*

But that didn't stop him making an absolute mint out of surgical appliances. And Lady Basil, your family returned from Australia in triumph, as great landowners, where they had gone in shame and ignominy.

The other GUESTS *stare at her amazed.*

So fitting, isn't it, that sheep should get them into trouble and out of it again? So I know this is only the beginning for me. And if in the distant future I was ever to receive by some act of mindless generosity on the part of people up whose shoelaces I'm not worthy of doing, say a knighthood or maybe a humble CBE for starters, then I would truly know that I had arrived.

The GUESTS *are gobsmacked.*

But who am I to stand here talking about knighthoods or even peerages maybe, to reward my work with the homeless – Lord Singer of Notting Hill, the whole idea is ridiculous – and yet, you know, at the same time: why not? Who's to say I'm not as good a person as the next person – I mean at least my ancestors weren't criminals, were they? Or Irish Micks who couldn't even get a potato to grow in their paddy fields?

SINGER *is looking at* LADY BASIL *and* LORD EARNER.

So anyway, thanks a million to all of you, all my friends, and especially Lord Bunty for putting in a word for me with your brother at the Home Office. I drink to you all.

The GUESTS *all stare accusingly at* BUNTY.

SINGER *drinks to them all.*

MANIK *and* STEFAN *applaud.*

The others stand in silence.

And now let's have some fun!

SINGER *cues the* BAND *who start to play 'Rock Around the Clock'.*

LORD EARNER *speaks over the band.*

LORD EARNER. Actually, actually time marches on, Singer.

The BAND *fizzles out.*

SINGER. What? But we're going to boogie the night away!

LORD EARNER. Some other time perhaps.

PEPPER *and* SHALLCROSS *step forward with* MRS DALEY.

MRS DALEY. Peter Singer? I've got something for you.

She throws her drink in SINGER's *face.*

This man threw my husband and me onto the streets and our belongings after us.

SINGER. What? Evict an old lady? Me.

MRS DALEY. My husband died of a broken heart because of you.

SINGER. So you have no witnesses? How dare you come in here with these outrageous accusations. Call the police!

A SERVANT *goes off to call the police.*

MRS DALEY *looks to* PEPPER *and* SHALLCROSS *for support.*

PEPPER. We've got signed statements from other tenants, Singer!

SHALLCROSS. Sworn affidavits! Your reign of terror is coming to an end!

SINGER. What? (*To* MRS DALEY). Dear lady, there is an apartment over my garage. I would like you to take it, rent-free, until this case is thoroughly investigated.

MRS DALEY. I wouldn't live under your roof if it were the last place on earth. This man as good as killed my husband!

LORD EARNER. This is too sordid. Goodbye, Singer.

The guests start to leave.

SINGER. You've gone too far now. Get out, get out. Manik. Throw them all out.

MANIK *steps forward.*

MRS DALEY. And this man here strangled my dog!

There is a stunned silence. The GUESTS *look at* MANIK *with horror-struck faces.*

LORD EARNER. Killed a dog? Is this true, Singer?

SINGER. Why ask me? Anyway, what's a dog?

LORD EARNER. What's a dog!

LADY BUNTY. Is it true? You strangled a poor defenceless little dog?

MANIK. Stone the crows. Uncle Peter, what should I say?

LADY BUNTY *throws her drink over* MANIK.

SINGER. Just say it isn't true.

MANIK. It isn't true. It wasn't a little dog it was a bloody big dog.

SIR BASIL. Whipping's too good for him.

MANIK. Whipping?

LORD EARNER. Killing a dog's a criminal offence. He should go to prison. Have you reported this to the police, dear lady?

MANIK. Prison?

MANIK *starts to back away.*

PEPPER *and* SHALLCROSS *restrain him.*

PEPPER. Hold him tight, Shallcross.

SHALLCROSS. The game's up, Singer.

LORD EARNER. Did you know about this?

SINGER. Me? Of course not. Manik. *Say it isn't true*!

MANIK. Uncle Peter, you were there.

SINGER. What? What are you saying?

MRS DALEY. He bit it. He bit my dog. There was blood on his face.

Revulsion among the GUESTS. *They all look to* SINGER.

SINGER. You see, this is the unfortunate result of my kindness in employing a mental defective, a German mental defective, Lord Earner. I beg you to believe – ask yourself could I possibly do anything so . . . so *bestial*?

LORD EARNER. He did it on your behalf then? You're admitting that?

SINGER. It won't happen again. Believe me, big changes are on the way.

LORD EARNER. They most certainly are.

LORD EARNER *starts to leave, as do the other* GUESTS.

MANIK. Uncle Peter . . .

The POLICE *start to arrive.*

SINGER. Don't talk to me, you bloody freak! Come back, come back. All right, go. Go you bloody toffee-nosed bastards! Earner, I screwed your wife.

LORD EARNER (*as he goes*). Yes, I know.

MANIK. I will not have prisons.

The GUESTS *are all gone.*

Three POLICEMEN *confront* MANIK.

MANIK *flips. He takes* PEPPER's *fingers and tears the hand apart. He pulls* SHALLCROSS's *ear off.*

The POLICEMEN *beat him unconscious with truncheons as the* MUSICIANS *and* SERVANTS *scatter, leaving the stage.*

SINGER. Don't hit him! Please don't hit him!

Scene Three

Hampstead Heath, night, near water.

SINGER *walks forward at a snail's pace.*

MANIK *is led across the stage in a strait-jacket.*

SINGER *watches him go.*

STEFAN *comes on.*

Silence. Light shimmering on water.

STEFAN. I have to go with Manik.

SINGER. Yes. Help him if you can.

SINGER *gives* STEFAN *his wallet.*

There's some money. All I have. Everything else belongs to other people. Even my home. I only borrowed it for a while.

STEFAN. Peter. I'll come back later. There's a lot to say.

SINGER. No. Nothing to say.

STEFAN (*shakes his head, disagreeing*). The journey back is a long one. None of us takes the same path.

SINGER. Stefan, how did you keep hold of your life? How?

Off stage an engine starts up.

STEFAN. I have to go. I'll be back.

STEFAN *goes. The sound of a van leaving.*

Silence. Water lapping. Music can be heard now from the house.

SINGER. God. The bread I broke with Manik was more than bread. Wasn't it? No answer? No explanation? Then go to hell, God, and I'll see you there.

SINGER *removes his clothes.*

It was our parents who were fooled. they thought the world had changed and didn't listen to their parents. Nat knew better than Josef. Marja knew better than Pesa. 'This is the twentieth century now. We belong here. Lvov is ours. We are not guests in another man's home. We live freely, without fear and without disguise.' It never occurred to them.

It's cold. So cold. So cold.

SINGER *walks into the water.*

I'm worthless. Worthless. I am nothing.

SINGER *disappears slowly into the water as he speaks.*

My name was Piotre Singer. I began in Lvov in 1919. I came to London in the South East of England, where I bought houses. I made a lot of deals. I ate a lot of shit, but never German shit. My life was a waste of time because I am worthless. I ended in 1960 in a pond in Hampstead while fish blinked patiently among the reeds.

ACT FOUR

Enter CHORUS, *with a suitcase and spare boots.*

CHORUS. To you queuing for a drink at the bar or a seat in the
ladies' loo it seems like twenty years have passed but here it's
only eight. Singer walked off the earth and into a watery grave.
So it was said – but no body was ever found and for months
afterwards people swore they saw Singer. Singer in his Rolls;
Singer at the opera; Singer in a crowd, always looking
ferociously alone. Of course nobody could ever get to him,
reach him, talk to him, actually touch the ghost of Singer, and
yet, and yet. But as we know: people see what they want to see.
After a while we heard no more of Singer. But 'Singerism' took
his place – the idea of him more famous than ever flesh and
blood had been. A government fell; washed up, wanked out,
tarred with the brush of our man's name; another climbed
unsteadily into office. Too long in the wilderness to bear a hint
of scandal anywhere on its own benches and with a mighty
stick to beat the old guard.

Singerism, noun: extortion or exploitation by landlords of
tenants of dilapidated or slum property, especially involving
intimidation against sitting tenants and violence against dumb
animals. Singerism: a disease. Singerism: wickedness, greed,
evil. Eight years and a whole world have passed.

He picks up his suitcase, sadly, wearily.

Now the white heat of technological revolution dazzles the
eyes and all the youth of England are on fire.

Scene One

*A squat. A giant bed. Underneath a cover, many sleeping forms, male and
female. Loud snoring.*

Enter SINGER, *through the audience. Older, hairier, but dressed well. He talks to the audience.*

SINGER. Who said Jews don't make good swimmers? We make good everything. Lampshades, fertilisers, handbags. Why? For what reason was it done to us? For years I tried to not want to know.

Now: for eight years I've asked the question every day. I want to know. There has to be an explanation. I cannot die until I hear it. I'm dead already, so they say, and evil. Strange! I never saw myself as a bad man when I lived but when I died I read so much about my wickedness – how I tore babies from their mothers' nipples and threw them onto the streets, went through widows' waterworks with a chainsaw; fed all week on caviar from between a famous whore's legs while my tenants ate Kit-E-Kat sandwiches and slashed their wrists on rent day. So be it. It starts to grow on you this Singerism. They say the only good Jew is a dead one. But who says a dead Jew has to be good? And what law is it that forbids a dead man from seeking revenge?

Enter STEFAN.

Stefan. Is this the place? Let's start our work.

STEFAN. I understand you have some paintings for sale! Raus! Raus! Wake up!

The THREE MEN *and* FOUR WOMEN *in the big bed are startled out of sleep and into their clothes. It's a real pantomime.*

COLIN. It's a bust!

OTHERS. Oh, no, what a drag! What time is it? If it's my father, the answer's the same! I'm not supposed to be here! Why can't they leave us in peace!?

DEREK *stumbles to the window and sees* SINGER.

DEREK. Oh, shit! There's two of them! We're surrounded! Flush everything down the bog!

JANICE. I don't want to go to prison!

DENISE. I want my mother and I want her now!

JANICE. If we're talking tear gas, deal me out!

An amazing amount of drugs is taken out from various places and piled up in the middle of the room.

COLIN. Shit, man, let's fight it out once and for all . . .

ELLIE. No. Let's chuck it down the bog, quick!

Someone takes it all out and flushes it away.

DEREK. Come and get us, you bastards!

SINGER. Calm yourselves. I'm the owner of a little art gallery. My name is Peter Godunov.

They pause as this sinks in.

DEREK. How many of you are there?

SINGER. Two. Boy, a college education, eh?

PAUL. How do we know you're not the fuzz?

SINGER. You don't get Jewish fuzz! We can't work Saturday. There'd be nobody patrolling the touchline at Arsenal.

COLIN. I know! It's the Day Long Group Mind Merger Bloke!

SINGER. I'm just a man who wants to buy paintings.

PAUL. Art For Sale is a bourgeois concept.

SINGER. I've brought cash.

All the students, except RUBY *and* PAUL *fall over themselves to line up with paintings.*

SINGER *and* STEFAN *go in.*

SINGER *starts to examine the canvasses.*

PAUL *reluctantly brings out some vivid specimens of his own.*

Which one is she?

STEFAN *(indicating* RUBY*)*. Over there.

SINGER. What's your name?

COLIN. Colin.

SINGER. Colin. *(He pats his face warmly.)* You have talent. I'll buy them both. Shall we say twenty pounds?

He pays him. He moves on to JANICE.

You're gifted. This one I must have.

He gives her ten pounds. He moves on to DENISE. *He stands awestruck. He gasps.*

SINGER. What's your name?

DENISE. Denise.

SINGER. Denise. What do people say, Denise, when you show these canvasses?

DENISE. They usually say, 'What the fuck's it mean?'.

SINGER. 'What the fuck's it mean'!?

He shakes his head in disbelief.

Philistines! Don't they know: the medium is the message. Right? McLuhan said it all. I'll take the lot. (*He pays her.*)

PAUL. Friend of yours, is he?

SINGER. Who – Marshall. Difficult man to get to know. But worth it. Same with Kerouac, you know? This is fabulous! (*He's holding* ELLIE*'s painting.*)

PAUL (*pursues him*). What – you sayin' you know Kerouac as well? Jack Kerouac?

SINGER *is apparently too engrossed in* ELLIE*'s painting to reply.*

PAUL. What did you say your name was? You've got a familiar face!

ELLIE. Look, stop hassling him, will, you? He's trying to look at my paintings.

SINGER. Incredible. Almost beyond words!

He moves on to DEREK*'s paintings before he has bought* ELLIE*'s.*

Now words fail me.

He moves on to PAUL*'s paintings. He barely glances at them.*

These I find rather trivial.

He turns back to the others.

But I'll take all of the others! All of them!

General rejoicing. He turns his sights on RUBY.

What about you? No paintings?

RUBY. Not for sale, I'm afraid.

SINGER. I can't imagine that's true.

RUBY. That says something about your imagination.

The STUDENTS *laugh.*

COLIN. Ruby's our sort of . . . patroness.

PAUL. Don't talk shit all your life, Colin. Have a day off.

DEREK. Well she pays for everything, doesn't she?

SINGER. Is this true, Miss Gailunas?

RUBY. How do you know my name?

SINGER *is caught out.*

STEFAN. It's on the doorbell.

PAUL. I've never noticed it.

SINGER. That's what's missing in your painting, my friend: the observant eye.

JANICE. All art is observation, Paul.

SINGER. All art is bourgeois crap! Unless it takes as its subject the class struggle. Even these canvasses, magnificent though they are, could be misread by the untrained eye, if seen isolation. But to me they smack of a very great struggle.

JANICE. We're a performance art group, er . . .

SINGER. Peter.

ELLIE. The paintings are all connected to the show.

SINGER. What's it called?

DEREK. 'The Theory And Practice Of Global Nightmare.'

SINGER. That I'd like to see.

JANICE. Well it's not really ready.

SINGER. That's a pity – you see, my gallery has a little performance space . . .

COLIN. I mean this is like our preliminary statement about . . . well everything.

SINGER. Why go for less?

COLIN. It's the whole capitalist mess. It's fascism. It's Vietnam.

SINGER. Yes!

COLIN. It's . . . It's a lot of personal shit I've had from my mum and dad, it's . . . it's . . .

PAUL. It's the whole mess, man! It's Singerism!

Silence.

SINGER *looks at* STEFAN.

STEFAN. He was a famous landlord. A wicked bastard.

PAUL. We'll show you.

SINGER. Please.

They all go, except SINGER, RUBY *and* STEFAN.

PAUL. Are you coming, Ruby?

RUBY. In a minute.

He goes.

SINGER. Your friend doesn't like me.

RUBY. 'Friend' would be going too far. We just screw.

SINGER. Ah. It sounds a little joyless.

RUBY. It's a bodily function. Three times a day like food.

SINGER. No wonder he has no energy for his art.

STEFAN. Maybe he's chasing your money, Ruby.

RUBY. In that case he'd be better off screwing my father. Well
. . . on second thoughts . . .

SINGER. Your father's in business maybe?

RUBY. Was. Other people run it now. He's what's politely known
as an eccentric. A recluse.

SINGER. What – he *never* goes out?

RUBY. That's what a recluse is.

STEFAN. So he stays at home now and *spends* his money. On you.

SINGER. On whatever makes you happy.

RUBY. Sort of.

SINGER. And what makes you happy, Ruby?

She thinks about it.

RUBY. Fucking. Really.

SINGER *and* STEFAN *nod silently.*

SINGER. And what does your father think of that?

RUBY. He knows I live my own life.

SINGER. Are you saying you don't get on with your father? That would be a shame.

RUBY. We get on fine.

SINGER. That's good.

RUBY. I'm all he cares about.

Pause.

SINGER. I see. That's wonderful.

He glances at STEFAN.

RUBY. I just don't understand the obsession with guilt, death, and all the other shit that generation got itself into.

They are taken aback. Is she talking about them? They recover.

SINGER. So he feels guilty, your father? Why's that? Because he's rich. Yeh, that's very English. Oh, but he's not English. He can't be, surely, with a name like Gailunas?

RUBY. Ukrainian.

STEFAN. What could your father be guilty of, Miss Gailunas?

SINGER. Exactly what I was wondering, Stefan.

RUBY. The guilt of the survivor.

SINGER. Survivor?

RUBY. He was in a camp.

SINGER. He has told you this?

RUBY. Yeh. He was a prisoner in a camp. Auschwitz.

SINGER. Well, well. That's too bad. Isn't it, Stefan?

STEFAN. Many people died in that camp.

RUBY. But he didn't. He feels guilty because better men than him died. I think. I don't know. He won't talk about it. It's hard for him, I suppose, but . . . I wish . . .

STEFAN. Yes. It's hard for him. Speak, Peter.

SINGER. Yes. Terrible for him. Stefan.

Silence.

PAUL (*off*). Ruby, are you coming or not?

She starts to go. She turns to SINGER.

RUBY. I'll see you later, Peter.

She gives him a very frank smile.

SINGER. Yes. That would be nice, Ruby.

She goes.

STEFAN *is rooted to the spot.*

SINGER *claps his hands with joy.*

STEFAN. A prisoner in the camp.

SINGER. Everything falls into place.

STEFAN. She's beautiful.

SINGER. I'll have the daughter, and then I'll have the father. But first: 'The Theory And Practice Of Global Nightmare'. Do I have time to purchase a small carton of Maltesers?

SINGER goes off front of stage as the lights change and the PERFORMERS *prepare to perform.*

Music on a harmonium.

SOMEONE *sells* SINGER *some sweets.*

SINGER *sits in the audience sharing his Maltesers and his wit and wisdom.*

Have a Malteser. Pass them round. I've never seen this avant-garde theatre but I've heard a lot about it. God, I hope the women take their clothes off, don't you? Do you play tennis? God, I hope there's none of that audience participation. I don't know about you, I could cringe. Whoops, it's starting. Settle down. Give it a chance, that's all I'm asking.

A song in multi-part harmony accompanied by the harmonium. A scene set against an animated back-projection: a series of landscapes each giving way in succession to something more threatening as the song gives way from soft and peaceful to harsh and loud. The end is a nightmare. PAUL *begins by walking in peaceful green countryside. This gives onto a street, an alleyway, a train, a tunnel; out of the tunnel comes the zebras and the walker is in the laager.*

PAUL (*singing*).
    Flesh and blood or shadows?
    Can this really be a man?
    He doesn't really understand his situation.
    He was born.
    And saw the Road to Heaven
    This much is true.

    Pity the poor immigrant
    With a price on his soul
    Never really master of his situation
    He was born
    And saw the Road to Heaven
    This much is true.

    How's he gonna get them out?
    Throw them on the streets.
    Now he's got an Empire
    of slums across the nation.

    Then at last he's British. Not homeless any more.
    We'll throw a party big as Selfridges,
    a celebration.

    Lungs slowly filled with water
    Floating arse up to the moon.
    What's the truth of the situation?
    The singer died
    And took the Road to Heaven
    Can this be true?

    Flesh and blood or shadows?
    Can these really be men?

The ZEBRAS *appear walking at a snail's pace.*

SINGER *cries out.*

    Does he really require an explanation?
    He was born
    He took the Road to Heaven
    And still he asks 'what's true'?

    Only this is true.
    Nothing else is true.

Silence.

SINGER *gets on stage and touches the* ZEBRAS. *One of them is*
RUBY.

RUBY. You're shaking.

SINGER. It was so powerful.

DEREK. You enjoyed it then?

SINGER. Enjoyed? I'm crazy about it. I'm in love with your minds.

RUBY (*to* SINGER, *quietly*). You were there, weren't you?

SINGER looks at her but doesn't reply.

DENISE. Paul knows all there is to know about Singer.

SINGER. But I know you writers – you get all your best ideas out of other people's books.

PAUL. I was *there*, man. My old man was his first tenant. I was just a baby. There was this horrible smell –

SINGER. Ivanhoe!

PAUL (*to* STEFAN). I bet you never knew he started in a camp.

RUBY. That's why he deserves some pity.

PAUL. Pity's a bourgeois concept. The guy was depraved. Full stop.

SINGER. And yet he took your family off the streets and put a roof over your heads. Don't you think that somewhere even in the darkest heart there is . . . ?

Not a flicker from PAUL.

PAUL. Let's get cleared up.

They start to clear the set away.

STEFAN pulls SINGER aside.

STEFAN. Let's forget this, Peter. Let's go home.

SINGER. Home? Where's that?

RUBY comes to them.

RUBY. So you don't want the show. I don't blame –

SINGER. Of course I want it. Pack it up. Get it in the van. Here's the address.

Rejoicing.

He gives PAUL *the address on a card. He takes out a roll of money and holds it out to* PAUL.

Just one question. So what was the meaning of it all? What was the explanation?

PAUL. No meaning, man. No explanation. 'The medium was the message.'

He leaves the stage with the others.

SINGER *and* STEFAN *are alone.*

SINGER. No explanation, eh? We'll see about that. (*He finds this hard to bear.*)

STEFAN. Do you want my advice?

SINGER. No. Isn't she an angel? Ruby Gailunas is already planning the moment when she'll open her legs for me.

STEFAN. She's happy. Hasn't there been enough suffering?

SINGER. Not yet. Don't you want to meet Gailunas one more time? To ask him a question? Say you don't, Stefan, and we'll leave now.

STEFAN (*after a while*). Yes. I want to meet him. To ask him a question.

SINGER. So you're not a saint after all.

STEFAN. No, I'm not a saint. But don't you think the girl is innocent of her father's crimes?

SINGER. As innocent as your mother and mine were. Free in her heart and happy. but she's *all he cares about in the world*. Therefore . . .

RUBY *sings off stage.*

RUBY. Pity the poor immigrant with a price on his soul.

She enters.

Peter?

SINGER. How do I look, Stefan? Like a lover?

He leaves with her.

STEFAN. Revenge is wrong. I know it's wrong. And yet: to see that face again. That head that never bowed except to watch children pass by on the Road to Heaven. To look him in the eye where once we dared not look on pain of death and ask him, 'Why?'. So. Peter will make the daughter burn and then smoke out the father.

He leaves.

Scene Two

STEFAN's *studio. Sun is streaming in through the skylight.*

RUBY *is listening to* SINGER *who is singing in the bath, off. She breaks off from setting a table for tea.*

RUBY. Sunday. Bright and cold. Last night we talked. Before we talked we made love. Before that, night fell. Before that we talked and before that another day broke bright and cold and another night fell. But first of all and last of all and the first night of all we made love. I can taste him in my mouth. I can smell him on my hair. Feel his breath on my back and see the prints my fingertips left on the wall as I balanced to take him into me. I can still hear his story about a world he used to know, a man he used to be, and the place his life was changed. Now at last I know more than the name of that place. And now those things in my father's life which never made sense before begin to make sense and I can start to understand my own life. It's a story I should've been told before. In the night Peter wept and wished I could've met that man he used to be. But I couldn't love that man more than I do this.

SINGER *sighs heavily in his bath, like a lost lover.*

STEFAN *enters softly.*

RUBY *finishes laying the table for tea.*

STEFAN *is plainly astonished. He can hear* SINGER *singing, off.*

STEFAN (*to* RUBY). Peter?

RUBY. Yes. He woke up and wanted a bath.

STEFAN. Woke up?

RUBY. Yes.

STEFAN. From sleep?

RUBY. Yes.

STEFAN. Peter was asleep?

RUBY. Yes.

STEFAN. Did he dream?

RUBY. Yes, I think he did. He smiled. He dreamt of something good, I think.

STEFAN. Yes. Of something better than death.

RUBY. Well, I expect so, Stefan. You talk about death the way some people talk about the weather.

She laughs.

He smiles, bashfully. He's charmed by her.

STEFAN. You are right. Too much of death.

RUBY. I want us to be friends. Can we be friends?

He doesn't answer. He stares at her.

She surprises him with a kiss on the cheek.

SINGER *arrives just in time to see it.*

SINGER. Ay, ay, already she's deceiving me!

STEFAN *laughs.*

Stefan? Laughing? Here. Sit. Are you OK?

He sits STEFAN down with mock concern.

RUBY. More.

SINGER. More what?

RUBY. More everything. For all time.

She goes to the door.

SINGER. You're going out?

RUBY. I'll be back soon. With a surprise.

SINGER. Promise.

RUBY. Promise.

SINGER. Soon?

RUBY. Very soon.

SINGER. Sooner than very soon.

RUBY. Very, very soon.

She goes.

SINGER *sighs heavily and gazes after her. He sees* STEFAN *looking at him sternly. He smiles.*

STEFAN. How much longer are you going to wait?

SINGER. Don't preach at me!

STEFAN. But, Peter – !

SINGER. I don't want to hear it!

STEFAN. Peter – !

SINGER. I'm in love! Is that such a crime?!

STEFAN. Then perhaps it's a sign. Time for you to wipe the slate clean and forget.

SINGER. Forget?

STEFAN. It was a freak of history –

SINGER. You're saying forget?

STEFAN. A small moral landslip that turned into an avalanche. Why ask a piece of ice why it took part in an avalanche?

SINGER. This is *Stefan* telling *me* to forget?

STEFAN. You could go away with her. She need never know who you really are.

SINGER. And maybe we could marry and live happily ever after with tea on Sundays with my father-in-law and she need never know who *he* really is?!

STEFAN. But if we do this to her, poison her life with this filth, we deserve to be condemned.

SINGER. Condemned? Condemned by who?

STEFAN. Then how much longer are you going to wait?

SINGER. Don't preach at me! I'm in love!

STEFAN. Then go away with her and forget!

SINGER. Don't keep telling me to forget! Should I forget my mother and father? Should I forget Manik and what was done

to him? Forget what was done to us? You're Almighty Jesus
Christ now, are you, forgiving everybody's sins?!

Silence.

STEFAN. Then you will do it now? Today? When she comes
back. Ask her to bring her father.

SINGER. Just a day or two more. I can't help it, Stefan. It's gone
straight into my veins. I'm happy, God help me.

STEFAN. You really love this girl, Peter?

SINGER. Completely. Completely, Stefan.

STEFAN. Don't you see, Peter? You've found something better
than remembering or forgetting. One life, Peter. That's all.
Don't miss this chance of a little happiness. You don't have to
be alone anymore. Don't be like me.

SINGER. Stefan?

STEFAN. Go away with her. Why not?

SINGER *thinks about it. He looks at* STEFAN *with hope in his eyes.*

SINGER. I could. She thinks I'm a whole man. And so I am,
Stefan. She even wishes her father could be like me!

He's nearly there.

STEFAN. There's nothing to stop you, Peter. Quickly. Go and
pack two bags.

SINGER. Yes. Stefan, yes!

He starts to go. He sees the table. It's set for four. But only three chairs.
STEFAN *sees it too.*

What? Four places?

They hear the sound of a wheelchair approaching.

RUBY (*off*). Peter! Stefan! Eyes closed!

SINGER. Cold. Cold. Cold.

RUBY *wheels on* GAILUNAS. *A pathetic broken figure.*

STEFAN. It's him.

RUBY. Surprise! Peter. Stefan. My father.

Silence.

RUBY. Father, you sit here. Peter here and Stefan here.

She wheels him into place and makes the others sit. She pours them all tea. She offers the cake box with a flourish.

Ta ta! *Torte checovla dovee!*

SINGER. *Torte checovla dovee?*

RUBY. *Torte checovla dovee.* To remind you all of Poland.

Silence.

She cuts the cake into slices.

Silence.

Eat. Eat.

She puts cake in front of Gailunas.

Silence.

Well, shall we talk about the weather?

GAILUNAS. The weather is very cold.

SINGER *jumps out of his chair.*

SINGER. That voice. Cold. Cold. The weather is very cold.

GAILUNAS. What's the matter with him?

SINGER *recovers. He sits.*

Silence.

GAILUNAS. The weather is bright. But very cold.

Silence.

What's the matter with them, for God's sake? Which is the one you want to marry? This one? What are you?

SINGER. What am I?

GAILUNAS. What the hell is the matter with them? One says nothing at all. The other one only says what the last person said.

RUBY. Peter's an art collector, Father. I've told you. And Stefan paints.

GAILUNAS. I don't like art. It's a waste of time.

RUBY. Have some cake.

GAILUNAS. I don't want any cake. Can I go home now?

He hates this. He doesn't like being out.

RUBY takes the plunge.

RUBY. Father. Peter and Stefan were in the same camp as you.

GAILUNAS. What? How dare you?

He wheels himself away.

RUBY propels him back to the table.

RUBY. Father, you have to talk about it. Peter can talk about it. When you can talk about the camp, you'll finally leave it. Peter, please. Help him. Help him to face the past. Help him to be like you.

SINGER. What?

RUBY. Please. Eat, Stefan.

STEFAN can't move.

Silence.

SINGER. What should I call him?

RUBY. Antanas. Stefan, could you give him some tea – he can't manage.

STEFAN holds the cup for GAILUNAS to sip. He sips. He dribbles. STEFAN wipes him carefully. SINGER tries to drink but the cup and saucer dance about in his hands.

SINGER. So you were in Auschwitz. Antanas?

GAILUNAS doesn't reply.

RUBY urges SINGER on.

GAILUNAS. Go home now, Ruby.

RUBY. But you have had no cake. Father. Please, Father.

She puts some cake in front of him.

SINGER. I wonder if we could've been there at the same time. What was your number?

GAILUNAS. I can't remember.

SINGER. You've forgotten your number? Let me see if I can remember your face. It's familiar. Do you remember mine?

GAILUNAS. I saw a million faces. I don't remember individuals.

STEFAN. Look at mine. It's hardly changed. I was Blockchief for the children.

GAILUNAS *nearly dies.*

RUBY. Children?

GAILUNAS. No, there were no children when I was there.

SINGER. Eat, Antanas. Tell me, what did you do to get put in Auschwitz?

GAILUNAS. I . . . I resisted the Nazis.

STEFAN. Ah. Aaaah.

SINGER. So – you were a hero?

GAILUNAS. No, no, I'm not saying that. I –

SINGER *stuffs cake into* GAILUNAS's *mouth.*

SINGER. Eat, Antanas, eat. Eat your *checovla dovee.* So you don't remember us. Yet I have a feeling we met. What can we do to help, Stefan?

But STEFAN *is crying.*

RUBY *is worried about it all.*

RUBY. Stefan? What children? Peter, I don't understand what is happening. Stefan, are you all right?

SINGER. He'll be all right. Stefan. Stop. Stop crying.

STEFAN *stops.*

RUBY *looks at her father.*

RUBY. Father? He's frightened, Peter. Maybe it's enough for one day?

SINGER. Don't worry, Ruby. I'm going to help your father. Sooner or later Antanas will start remembering. All he needs is help. Antanas, do you remember Manik, a high number who couldn't live on the dumplings in his dreams, a red triangle who lost his shirt – no, the truth is he was cheated of his shirt, gave it away for a single piece of bread – and a prisoner was ordered to beat his head in –

GAILUNAS. No, no, I don't remember!

SINGER. I can still hear the crack of sticks on Manik's bare head, even now I hear it before I drop off to sleep. Stefan, what was the name of that guard who gave the order? You knew him well: you gave him children to sleep with so that we could stay alive.

RUBY *gags on rising vomit.*

He was Ukrainian, wasn't he, Stefan? What was his name? It's on the tip of my tongue.

RUBY. Ukrainian? (*It's dawning on her.*)

GAILUNAS. Home now, Ruby. Ruby. You want to marry this ridiculous old man and live in the past? Ruby?

SINGER. Old? Yes, I'm old, but I was never young. I got onto a train a young man who had never seen anybody die and I got off five days later an old man with death sewn into the lining of my clothes.

What was his name, Stefan? He was evil. I would say of any man I knew, he was evil. Wouldn't you say, Stefan?

RUBY. I don't agree.

SINGER (*taken aback*). What?

RUBY. I don't agree.

SINGER. Oh, you don't?

RUBY. No. I think those men – those camp guards – weren't supermen of any kind, not big men at all, not extraordinary men like you, Peter, capable of great kindness or great cruelty; there were just . . . ordinary.

GAILUNAS. That's right! Just ordinary men! Just ordinary men doing what they were told!

RUBY. We're going now, Father. It was a mistake.

SINGER. Oh, no, it wasn't ordinary. Believe me, Ruby, it wasn't ordinary. There was no order that said this man had to enjoy carrying out orders. No rule that said this man whose name is now on the tip of my tongue had to carry out the rules with enthusiasm.

RUBY. There's no such thing as evil.

SINGER. You're English, Ruby, English through and through – which is to say you have no idea of evil.

RUBY. I don't believe in it. There's no such thing as an evil man. What does evil look like? It's a ridiculous idea!

SINGER. I cannot tell you what evil looks like. It tastes like ice in your throat, it smells like piss going down your legs, and I know the sound: it's a voice that doesn't have to raise itself because it can never be opposed, it belonged to a man who could snuff out our lives any moment he felt like it and nobody in the world would know or care. (*He's shouting at* RUBY *now*.) Don't forgive! It's not your place to forgive!

Silence.

RUBY *knows now. She's rooted to the spot by his ferocity.*

Of course! Stefan! You painted that man. You see, Antanas, art has its purposes after all. I'm sure it will all come back to you when we show you that face.

SINGER *wheels him to the mural of faces, which* STEFAN *now uncovers.*

RUBY *gasps. There, in the middle, is* GAILUNAS *as he was.*

Silence.

GAILUNAS. Ruby. Ruby.

STEFAN. My name was Stefan Gutman. Every day you asked me for a list of children's names. These children were gassed and burnt.

RUBY. No. Please.

SINGER. My name was Peter Singer. Oh yes, Peter Singer. I was a human being. You turned me into nothing. I was solid, I was real. I demand to know the reason why. Why was that done to me?

Silence.

GAILUNAS *weeps.*

RUBY. Tell them what they want to know.

GAILUNAS. I can only tell you what I remember. And I'll tell you the truth. I'll do it for my daughter's sake and I'll swear it on her life.

He looks at STEFAN.

This man here I remember now. Little Blockchief. I remember you.

SINGER's *waiting. Nothing.*

SINGER. What about me? Me?

GAILUNAS. I swore to tell the truth. On my daughter's life. If you were there, then you were there. But I have no memory of you at all.

SINGER *can hardly take it in.*

SINGER (*quietly*). But you must remember me.

He goes to GAILUNAS.

STEFAN *has sat in a corner.*

You must remember me! You must remember me! You must remember me!

GAILUNAS *just stares at him, almost with pity.*

SINGER *desists.*

Silence.

ACT FIVE

Scene One

The South Bank in London.

Enter the **CHORUS**. *The* **CHORUS** *now dressed as a vagrant. As he speaks* **HOMELESS PEOPLE**, *young, old, male, female, slowly congregate.*

A **FIGURE** *swathed in an overcoat, scarf, hat and gloves, pushes on stage a mobile soup kitchen and dispenses bread and soup to the homeless, who seem to revere him. He is wearing a balaclava.*

CHORUS. Let nobody accuse us of not daring to dream. We gazed into the future – for a time were hypnotised by it like mice by snakes – but had at last – when rough winds blew the ship of state off course and oil sheikhs shook our pockets out – to say, 'OK, the future doesn't work'. Then came the winter of our discontent. Rubbish rotting in these streets cheek by jowl with unburned corpses. Red Wedge leeched on the corrupt and bloated body politic while the sick and elderly cried in vain for care. Our children crazed, lungs heavy, veins bursting with heady drugs. Nation, torn by faction, family torn apart, the very idea of it mocked. We had finally lost the peace. Then came the turn of the tide. The Great Housekeeper, with fox-like cunning, lion's strength and matching crocodile accessories, whose object was, no less, to change our souls. Now is hopelessness banished by pride in hard work: wild-eyed profligacy by calm thrift; sneering, slouching defiance by straight-backed, head-up respect for authority; and paraplegic bleeding-heart self-doubt by erect patriotism in a leaner, fitter land. On the run at last the whinging unemployed, on permanent holiday at the State's expense: the lazy, self-seeking, shiftless immigrants swamping our culture with ganja and halal; and banished to the sidelines, for temporary respite only while we ponder longer term solutions, rank upon rank of godless homosexuals tampering with little children on the rates.

Man will not give up the sullen apathy of dependence just because you ask him nicely. You have to rip the drip-feed from his arm and drag him to his feet – without his back against the wall he'll never know the sheer delight of personal achievements. But the triumph of Marks and Spencer over Marx and Engels isn't cheap. There's a price tag on Progress. Every man a man of property and houses are the first. If you've got property, you've got something. But pennies don't come from heaven, the Great Housekeeper says, they have to be earned on earth. Without the poor, how would the rich man know he was rich? Without the weak to put the frighteners on him a strong man loses his nerve and turns to sainthood. Bless you. God bless you.

The CHORUS *takes some soup and bread from the* MAN.

The MAN *sees a* YOUNG GIRL *shivering in an anorak and jeans. He takes off his balaclava and puts it on her; gives her soup and bread. We now see that the man is* SINGER. *He takes more bread and soup to the other* HOMELESS PEOPLE.

STEFAN *comes on.*

STEFAN. Who'd've thought it? He's a different man. Since the day a Sunday tea almost ended everything and made all questions of 'why' irrelevant, he's devoted himself to these people. If I hadn't seen it night after night with my own eyes – for twenty years now – I wouldn't have believed it possible. But it is – we can change.

Another MAN *has been watching from a distance. He now approaches.*

MAN. Is this the man they call St Peter of the South Bank?

STEFAN. If you're a journalist, he won't speak to you.

MAN. I'm told he hardly speaks a word to anyone. Has he taken a vow of some kind?

STEFAN. Who are you?

MAN. His efforts don't go unnoticed, that's all. Tell him.

STEFAN. He wouldn't be interested. He wants nothing from anyone. Only to be left in peace.

MAN. Remarkable. And you? I'm told you paint.

STEFAN. Correct.

MAN. But only one subject. The history of certain tragic events from the middle of the century.

STEFAN. Correct also.

MAN. I'm told by people who can appreciate such things that you have real talent.

STEFAN. Many people have talent. Talent is irrelevant in my case.

MAN. Their advice is that application of your talent to other subjects would help your career.

STEFAN. Career? You misunderstand. Everything must be recorded that can be recorded. Nothing must be forgotten. That's all.

MAN. But surely – ?

STEFAN. Thank you for your interest.

MAN. My friends would genuinely like to help.

STEFAN. Do your friends burn books? That would help.

MAN. You want us to burn books? All books?

STEFAN. I personally know of 104 books now in print which claim that the Holocaust never happened. Burn them and I'll paint landscapes.

MAN. Ah. No can do. Not in Britain. Freedom of speech and all that.

STEFAN. Of course.

MAN. Well, I'll be late for curtain up.

The MAN *dashes off towards the theatre.*

The HOMELESS *sing 'Nobody' by Bert Williams, unaccompanied.* SINGER *applauds them.*

An uproar, off.

A WOMAN *theatregoer runs on.*

The HOMELESS PEOPLE *settle down to sleep.*

WOMAN THEATREGOER. There's a very drunk man urinating from the walkway. He only just missed me.

STEFAN. Give him your coat. Take him home with you.

The WOMAN THEATREGOER *turns to* STEFAN.

WOMAN. Well look, aren't you paid to take care of this sort of thing?

STEFAN. No, actually, I'm not. Have you spoken to him?

WOMAN. My husband's trying to reason with him but he's very abusive.

STEFAN. You should never abuse a drunk.

WOMAN. Are you trying to be funny?

The DRUNKEN MAN *comes on carrying the* WOMAN'*s* HUSBAND *in a bear hug. The* HUSBAND *is screaming with fear. The* DRUNK *sees the sleeping* HOMELESS PEOPLE. *He lets go of the* HUSBAND. *The* DRUNKEN MAN *speaks in German throughout the following.*

DRUNK. Ssh! Ssssh! The little Jews are asleep. Don't wake them up. They're having a lie-in this morning.

The WOMAN THEATREGOER *and her* HUSBAND *escape from the stage, quickly.*

Stop or you'll be shot. You can't escape. Sssh! Sssh! Have a lie-in, little Jews. We're going to have a holiday soon.

We see now that the DRUNKEN MAN *is none other than* MANIK.

STEFAN. Manik?

MANIK. Quiet!

STEFAN. Oh.

MANIK. And when you wake up, we're going to eat. Oh, how we're going to eat.

SINGER *takes a cloth and washes the filth from* MANIK'*s face.*

STEFAN. Manik? It's us.

MANIK. Are we going to eat?

SINGER *brings him soup and bread.*

No money.

STEFAN. It's free.

MANIK *laughs and hands the food back.*

MANIK. Nothing is free.

STEFAN. Don't you know us, Manik? It's Stefan.

MANIK *removes his ragged coat and gives* SINGER *his ragged shirt. He puts his coat back on and takes the food. He eats and drinks. He stops and looks at* SINGER.

MANIK. You're my Uncle Peter.

STEFAN *and* SINGER *fall on him with laughter and tears.*

STEFAN. Eat, Manik, eat. Eat as much as you like. And sleep with us at our house. Eat and sleep and no work. We'll never be apart again.

They all go.

Scene Two

The studio. STEFAN *is working on two canvasses. One is of children's faces, the other of* MANIK *as he was.* MANIK *is asleep on a bench, muttering occasionally in German, dreaming of dumplings. Rain is beating on to the skylight. Water is dripping into a bucket.*

STEFAN. Perhaps human beings should have no memory. No past or future, only the dripping tap of the never ending present. Coming from nowhere, going nowhere, beginning and ending every second. How soothing it must be to forget. What good is memory to Manik? What good a picture of the man he was before? The past has flooded in and drowned half a life. He has no idea where he came from, how he got here. Only the camp. This is what will happen to me. One day Time will start to run backwards, and . . .

He can't bear these thoughts. MANIK *cries out.*

STEFAN. The past should stay in the past! But what would Peter say? I mustn't flinch. The past must be confronted so that it will never return.

He starts to paint again. Enter SINGER *with his soup kitchen. He checks* MANIK *before removing his wet outdoor clothes.*

STEFAN. Asleep. He ate like a horse. As usual.

SINGER *strokes* MANIK. *He looks at the children.*

STEFAN. This girl's face came to me clearly in a dream last night. She came in a consignment from the East. She only lived long

enough to be undressed and shaved. But suddenly I
remembered – just at the end of the painting. Look here.
There was a tiny thread hanging from the back of her coat.
Just there. You see? No detail will be forgotten, Peter.

SINGER *nods.* STEFAN *paints.* SINGER *comes downstage and
stands alone.*

SINGER. God. Dear, dear God, on whose face I hope to look one
day. OK, you got me out of a lot of trouble. OK, you answered
my prayers and let me find something better than death. But
I've done twenty years of sackcloth and ashes. The first Jewish
saint. Isn't that enough? What sort of a God are you? I mean I
know somebody's got to help the homeless and I can see you
must think it's very funny that it's me. Homeless people are
human beings. I can see that now. I admit it. I pity them from
the bottom of my heart. And I know what I did in the past was
wrong. But have I let myself in for a lifetime of saintliness –
because quite frankly I can't stand much more of it. I can't
walk down the street without people touching the hem of my
garments.

He sneaks a look at STEFAN *who smiles at him and goes back to his
painting.*

I'd give it up tomorrow but what would Stefan say? He's
pinned all his hopes on me. He's always believed in goodness.
It's OK for him: he's naturally good so naturally he believes in
goodness. To be honest there are times when I could kick him
and his devotion to the past. If you ask me it's just an excuse
for not living life to the full. He should've been born 500 years
ago – he could have passed his whole life building a tiny part
of the east wing of some ghastly cathedral. No offence. And
just when I was hoping for a sign from you that I might be
allowed out of the slammer for maybe just an occasional day
trip even – or preferably a night: twenty years without a
woman already – what happens? You bring back this German
speaking vegetable who's going to eat me out of house and
home if he doesn't kill me first during one of his seizures! I'm
ready to start living again, and what are you trying to tell me?
That I'm stuck in here forever with a demented mangelwurzel
and the Beatrix Potter of the Holocaust?! It's so DULL!

A crash of thunder overhead makes MANIK *wake up.* SINGER *looks
horrified at the wrath of God.* MANIK *crashes round the room, barking
commands in German.*

MANIK. Raus! Raus und Ruhe! Ihr konnt nicht entkommen. Wo ist Dein Hemd? Du brauchst ein Hemd! Was bist Du? Du bist ein Arschloch! Du bist ein stinkendes Arschloch! Du glaubst Du Kannst mich veralben. Zuruck in die Reihe und halt's Maul.

They get him settled down again.

SINGER. I was thinking, Stefan. There has to be a way of publishing all this.

STEFAN (*worried*). Publishing? But I've tried . . .

SINGER. Yes, yes, I know. But if we had money ourselves, enough to pay to have it all photographed and bound.

STEFAN. But we haven't. Anyway, it isn't finished. No point until it's finished.

SINGER. No. Of course not.

SINGER *is quiet.*

STEFAN. Peter, I know what you are thinking. You could make money. It's true you have a talent for it, but –

SINGER. Had. Had.

STEFAN. No, no, for you it is a second nature to make money.

SINGER. You think I still could?

STEFAN. Of course. But what is more important? Raising money to make books nobody wants to buy, or feeding the hungry and the homeless? Besides, so much to do, so many faces.

SINGER (*getting exasperated*). But if nobody wants them then what's the point? Stefcho, for 30 years now you've painted so that the past would never be forgotten in a world where people can't remember what they had for breakfast. A world where people have forgotten how to remember. A world where leaders can tell any lie and not be brought to book if they brazen it out. Make any promise, safe in the knowledge that it never need be honoured. Scandalous deceit in high places – which once upon a time would lead to a swift resignation, a last walk in the garden and a bullet in the temple – is now forgotten in a week. Who needs forgiveness or retribution in a world which has no memory? So . . . what good is it to paint?

STEFAN. What good?

SINGER. Stefan, even you are getting old now. It has to end some day. That's all I'm saying.

STEFAN is speechless.

SINGER. For god's sake, your life is draining away. And so is mine. So is mine.

STEFAN stands staring at him. Then he turns away to his paintings and stares at them. SINGER throws up his hands in exasperation.

SINGER. How about it, God?

A knock at the door. A letter comes through the box. SINGER opens it and reads:

SINGER. 'Dear Mr Singer, The Prime Minister has it in mind to recommend to Her Majesty that you receive a knighthood'.

They stand in silence. He reads on.

SINGER. And I'm invited to lunch. Me, I'm to have lunch with the Great Housekeeper in person. At Number Ten! Stefan. I'm going back into the real world again!

Scene Three

Number Ten Downing Street.

A noisy gathering. People come at SINGER from all sides.

MAN. Mr Singer. Welcome.

TIM BUNTY. Tim Bunty. Very great pleasure to meet you again, sir. Of course I was only a toddler. You used to do business with my father in the '50s. Lord Bunty. You knew him rather well.

SINGER. I knew your mother rather better.

TIM BUNTY. You played a lot of tennis. I used to watch you.

SINGER raises an eyebrow. Somebody offers him champagne. He's about to drink it greedily when ALMOND whips it away again.

ALMOND. He only drinks tap water. With a twist of lemon. It was in the Mail on Sunday.

DAWSON. I'll be very interested to hear your thoughts, sir.

SINGER *looks puzzled.*

CURBISHLEY. Has no-one told you? We're here to offer our thoughts on the housing crisis.

SINGER. Housing? I think perhaps a mistake of some kind.

DE KNOP *arrives.*

MAN. Let me introduce Nicholas de Knop, a fervent admirer of your career.

DE KNOP *grabs his hand and shakes it enthusiastically.*

DE KNOP. Your early career, that is, not all this later stuff. I studied your methods, as a youth. I modelled myself on you. Your picture was on my wall. I found out what you found out, but let's not go into that when we're here to talk about the poor homeless people. Let me see if I can phrase this nicely. In your day you were free, am I right, Mr Singer? May I call you Peter? Nobody went without a home because you were allowed to find a spot for the poorest man.

SINGER *is given a glass of water. He sips.*

ALMOND. Exactly. Set the landlord free of all these petty restrictions –

DAWSON. – such as fair rents –

CURBISHLEY. – and watch the private sector solve the problem. Surely you can see that, Mr Singer? Charity is a good thing, but is it enough?

ALMOND. You've highlighted a terrible social problem. In fact it's rather embarrassing for government.

SINGER *is beginning to get the idea. They are desperate to hear his opinions.*

DE KNOP. Look the bottom line is: why should anybody bust a gut to help the homeless unless there's a goddam profit to be made? You must be able to see that, Peter?

SINGER *sips his water. The last remark was met with great approval in the room. But what does the great man think? Silence.*

TIM BUNTY. Well? What do you think, sir?

SINGER *clears his throat. They all hold their breath.*

SINGER. I think. Nobody need be homeless.

Great relief. Enthusiasm among the businessmen.

MAN. That's very much in line with latest government thinking, Mr Singer.

DE KNOP. As I like to say, Peter, if it wasn't for all those poor homeless people, people like me would be out on the streets.

He laughs. SINGER *smiles.* RUBY *arrives.*

DE KNOP. Put that drink down and come and say hello to a living legend. Peter Singer. Ruby. My wife.

Silence. RUBY *and* SINGER *stare at each other.* SINGER *drains his glass and hands it to* DE KNOP.

DE KNOP. Oh. Right. Do you think you could manage to speak to him while I get us a drink?

DE KNOP *goes.*

SINGER. Your husband is an idiot.

RUBY. Oh, no. It's much worse than that. You're thinner.

SINGER. I never expected to see you again. How are you, Ruby?

She looks away. She can't answer that.

RUBY. I suppose this is a silly question after all this time: why?

SINGER. Oh, God . . . Did you ever manage to forgive me?

RUBY. Did you ever forgive me for being English?

SINGER. I'm having to change my opinion about the English. Times change.

RUBY. He's coming back. Help me, Peter.

SINGER. I can't. It's too late. No going back anymore. The world is moving on.

DE KNOP *arrives back. A fanfare plays.*

DE KNOP. She's arriving. Come on.

The gathering rushes off to hail the chief. RUBY *looks at* SINGER. *He straightens his shoulders and marches into the future. She watches him go, sadly.*

Scene Four

The studio. STEFAN *comes on with string and finishes tying up paintings into bundles.* MANIK *follows.* STEFAN *is humming happily.* MANIK *is trying in vain to keep in tune. He is happy that* STEFAN *is happy.* STEFAN *looks at his watch.*

STEFAN. He's been away all day. Some lunch it must be, eh? Manik? You can't really understand me, can you? Some lunch. Some lunch Peter's having.

    STEFAN *mimes eating.* MANIK *nods enthusiastically.*

STEFAN. No, no, you've just eaten. OK, I'll get you more soup in a jiffy. Just let me finish. Finished. Done.

He stands back and looks at his paintings, all stacked in bundles.

STEFAN. Done. Good. Come on. Come on.

But there is one painting left. Of MANIK *as he was.* MANIK *sees it and stares at it.* STEFAN *sees this.*

STEFAN. Manik –

He's interrupted by SINGER *arriving, elated.*

SINGER. Stefan? Stefan? Manik! Quick! Get the place tidied up. I want it spick and span. Get rid of all this junk. I have people arriving any minute. A business meeting, Stefcho! Come on, Manik!

He puts a broom into MANIK's *hands and starts him off.*

STEFAN. He wants to eat.

SINGER. He can eat when he's finished work. Stefan, what do you think? It's like the '50s again out there, but with the gloves off this time. A country looking to the future at last, not obsessed anymore with the past. My God, I have such a good feeling again!

    MANIK *is staring at his portrait.*

SINGER. Manik, work! Get on with it! Twenty years of giving out soup, I forgot what it was like to feel the blood in my veins!

He looks at STEFAN's *face.*

SINGER. Well. You look like a man with something to say. OK. Go ahead.

STEFAN. No.

SINGER. No? You should rejoice, if you were a real friend.

STEFAN. Who are these people you've invited to our house?

SINGER. People who accept me for what I am. You should do the same. Manik, if you cannot be useful, go into the kitchen and stay there. Well?

STEFAN. Peter. Things are changing for you. That's good. For me too.

SINGER. Yah? What happened to your paintings?

STEFAN. I've thought it over what you said. You were right. It's finished.

SINGER. What – no more paintings?

STEFAN. No more paintings. This was the last. For Manik. Manik, for you. With all my heart.

He gives the painting to MANIK.

SINGER. And now? What now?

STEFAN. I have decided to go. Here's a letter. Read it when you have time.

He hands him a letter.

SINGER. Go? I see. Well. So be it.

RUBY *comes in. She drains the last from a half bottle of scotch, delicately. She looks at the room and at* STEFAN.

RUBY. You've had the decorators in.

STEFAN. Ruby?

RUBY. Peter and my husband are going into business. Won't that be wonderful? I'll bake another cake. Stop him, Stefan.

SINGER. Don't talk about me as if I'm not here.

RUBY. You got old, Stefan.

STEFAN. I have to go. Goodbye.

Enter DE KNOP, DAWSON, CURBISHLEY, TIM BUNTY *and* ALMOND.

DE KNOP. Now then, Mr Special Adviser on Housing Policy to the Prime Minister, I salute you! If there are men like us around who've made money out of houses it's because we stood on giant's shoulders.

RUBY. That's my husband. Now will you do something?

ALMOND. Tell us, Peter. What did you talk about at lunch? Everybody wanted to eavesdrop, but nobody could. You and the PM were that close, that intimate.

SINGER. Oh, this and that. Mainly post war British housing policy.

DE KNOP. Do you believe that, Ruby? You're a woman. Where is she?

RUBY. She was charmed, Nicholas.

DE KNOP. Charmed?

RUBY. Seduced maybe.

The other men laugh.

DE KNOP. I think my wife's a little bit charmed as well.

CURBISHLEY. Or is it seduced?

TIM BUNTY. Nicky's wife's been around the track a few times, Peter.

SINGER. Your wife is unfaithful to you, Nicholas?

DE KNOP. Habitually. Incapable of fidelity. What is it about some women, Peter? What makes them betray us, eh?

SINGER. I don't know.

DE KNOP. Happy now you've seen where the great man lives?

RUBY. Ecstatic, thank you, Nicholas.

DE KNOP. You can go home then, can't you?

DAWSON. The stories people tell about Peter Singer and women. You really knew how to handle them, didn't you?

SINGER. Yes. Can we please talk business?

DAWSON. Let's have a drink, shall we?

RUBY. At last.

SINGER. And talk business.

DAWSON *opens a hamper and takes out champagne, glasses, food and cutlery.*

RUBY. Are you going to stand there, Stefan?

STEFAN. It's too late.

RUBY. Did he really love me?

STEFAN. Yes.

TIM BUNTY. Would you consider coming into partnership with all of us?

SINGER. But I'm just a theorist now. No capital.

CURBISHLEY. You don't need capital to make money out of housing. All you need is access to other people's capital.

DE KNOP. You taught us that. Anyway, I'm made of money. I married it.

STEFAN. Gailunas' money, Peter.

SINGER. I thought you made your choice? Why don't you go? You don't fit in here anymore. What's your proposition, gentlemen? Where's the market these days?

MANIK *is holding his painting and staring at it.*

MANIK. Is this the market?

SINGER. Will you get him out of here!?

ALMOND. We buy as many big, clapped out old properties as possible –

SINGER. That brings back memories.

DE KNOP. Of course it does. But there's two big differences these days, Peter. Firstly, it pays to look as if you're performing a public service. And secondly, we're not talking about a few end terraces – we're talking about tower blocks. Whole estates.

RUBY. Stefan.

MANIK (*to* DAWSON). Something to eat, comrade?

DAWSON. Get away from me! Who is this, Peter?

STEFAN. This is his home, not yours.

DE KNOP. It isn't as a matter of fact. It's mine. I bought it last week. You don't mind, do you, Peter?

SINGER. Business is business, God knows.

STEFAN. Peter. Give me five minutes, please. I'm asking you.

SINGER. What are we going to do with these tower blocks? You haven't said.

DAWSON. First things first, Peter. Are you in or out?

CURBISHLEY. We want to form a consortium. With Peter Singer's name at the top.

SINGER. I must have total control of the company. I would tolerate no interference.

The MEN *glance nervously at each other.*

DE KNOP. That's all negotiable, Peter. The important thing is: we want you.

SINGER. But what's the deal?

STEFAN. Five minutes. That's all I'm asking.

MANIK *shows his portrait to* ALMOND.

MANIK. I was a whole man once, comrade.

ALMOND. I'm not your comrade, comrade!

ALMOND *pushes* MANIK *away violently.*

SINGER. Look, five minutes. Say your piece then go and take him with you.

STEFAN *and* SINGER *go aside.*

STEFAN. Peter, you don't need their deals. You've done something with your life.

SINGER. No. Nothing.

STEFAN. For twenty years, you've given your life to –

SINGER. I've given nothing. I have nothing to give. You go through life being who you really are and people spit in your face. You give out stale bread and keep your mouth shut for twenty years and the world thinks you're a saint! Why? Because the world is interested in lies only and not the truth.

STEFAN. So this is a reason to go back to what you were.

SINGER. *Am!* What I *am!* It's what you've never been able to accept about me. You're the same as the rest of them – you're only happy when I'm denying what I really am. Because you shit yourself with fear when you think about the truth about what happened to us!

STEFAN. And what is the truth?

SINGER. The truth is the camp. Auschwitz was the truth! It taught me everything I needed to know about myself. That's where I, Peter Singer, was born. And you, Stefan Gutman brought me into the world!

STEFAN. The man I kept alive in the camp was a man I knew in Lvov when I was a boy. A man who was not much more than a boy himself. My whole family, especially my mother, adored him. But to me he was both a hero and an older brother. Nobody I had ever met knew more about art, music, theatre, as that man did. I would say I have never met anybody who had such a talent for life. In those days. The days before. When we were both whole human beings.

SINGER (*quietly*). It doesn't exist anymore, Stefcho. There is no time before.

STEFAN *nods.* RUBY *has been listening.*

STEFAN. Then goodbye, Peter. Anyway, what the hell is wrong in feeling the blood in your veins, eh? Why worry? Nothing matters eh? Friend.

SINGER. Friend.

STEFAN *wants to embrace, but* SINGER *rejoins the businessmen.* STEFAN *kisses* MANIK. STEFAN *leaves quickly.* MANIK *watches him go. So does* RUBY. *She now gives up. She sits on* MANIK's *bench and drinks.*

SINGER. Now. Now then. Out with it. Who's going to live in these big clapped out towers we're going to buy?

They hesitate. It's crunch time. They look at BUNTY.

TIM BUNTY. Mental invalids.

SINGER. What?

MANIK. Something to eat, comrade? I'm hungry now.

TIM BUNTY. To begin with. That's the most urgent problem.

CURBISHLEY. They're letting them out on the streets and shutting down the bins.

ALMOND. They've got to go somewhere.

SINGER. Yah, I see that. It's like the schwarzers after the war.

TIM BUNTY. But that's just the tip of the iceberg, Peter. Think ahead. Have you any idea how many homeless people there are in London?

DAWSON. People shouldn't have to deal with these people in a face to face situation.

ALMOND. They should be off the streets and not making bloody nuisances of themselves.

DE KNOP. They need to be encouraged to get back on the ladder of home ownership. These camps would be the first step back –

SINGER. Camps?

CURBISHLEY. That's a bad word, Nicky. But certainly there's no point housing these social misfits if they're then free to wander back into the night whenever they please.

DE KNOP. There would have to be discipline. We all have to face up to that. Troublemakers would have to be dealt with.

SINGER. In what way?

ALMOND. These are details. The important thing is to get the operation up and running.

TIM BUNTY. That's where you come into it, Peter. We'd like to call the first settlement 'Sir Peter Singer Hamlets'. People trust you. Your name would bring investment – public and private – and would reassure the people we want to attract to live there.

SINGER. I see. But this 'discipline' . . ?

DE KNOP. Peter, It's got all the hallmarks of classical Singerism and it supports government policy into the bargain.

SINGER. You said 'discipline'.

ALMOND. The government needs a creative answer to the problem. Are you in or out?

SINGER. Yes, I can see that. 'Sir Peter Singer Hamlets'. But, I don't know . . .

They are getting very worried about him.

TIM BUNTY. What's this? Doubts, Peter?

SINGER. Well, I suppose, . . . Ruby? What do you think?

RUBY. I think once you've been in one of these places it's very hard to ever get out again. Goodbye, Peter.

She goes.

DE KNOP. Well? In or out?

Silence.

CURBISHLEY. He's lost his nerve.

DE KNOP. He just needs time to think.

ALMOND. He's a busted flush, Nicky. I told you he would be.

TIM BUNTY. He's too old.

DAWSON. Not the man you were, eh, Singer?

Silence from SINGER.

DE KNOP. Don't let me down, Peter.

SINGER. I feel cold. Cold.

DE KNOP. For Christ's sake, man, get a grip on yourself! These are the laws of life. Singerism is for all time and this is pure Singerism. The country's ready for it. If men of goodwill refuse to grapple with such urgent social problems instead of giving soup to lazy bastards who frankly should be made to work with bastinado then what's the future for this septic isle when even the silver sea we're set in's now polluted by slicks of dusky clothing manufacturers from Uganda setting up sweatshops in Birmingham with generous government grants, the channel approaches choking so-to-speak with armadas of boat people who couldn't make a go of it in easy-going Vietnam but think they'll have more luck with relatives in the Rickmansworth area! Why oh why does all the flotsam and jetsam of five continents wash up on our once golden beaches? I'll tell you why: because we were a soft touch to the niggers and the Jews!

Silence.

TIM BUNTY. If this isn't you, Singer, then what are you?

SINGER. What am I? What am I?

MANIK (*to* SINGER). I'm starving, comrade.

    SINGER *turns to him.* MANIK *is clutching his portrait.*

MANIK. Is this the market?

SINGER. What have you got, Manik?

MANIK. I'm not Manik, comrade. I have a coupon somewhere. I gave my spoon for it yesterday. I was cheated. I need a friend, comrade.

SINGER. Not Manik? Who then? Who are you? What's your name?

MANIK. I dreamt all night of dumplings. One bite of bread, comrade. I'm here because I spoke out for you people. I'm starving, comrade. What about my shirt?

SINGER. What's your name? Remember your name.

MANIK. My name? What does my name matter anymore?

SINGER. But what is it?

    MANIK *thinks.*

MANIK. My name? Otto Vanselow. From Dusseldorf.

SINGER. Otto Vanselow. From Dusseldorf.

    He hugs him. He gives him bread.

TIM BUNTY. Well, Singer? In or out?

SINGER. Out. Please leave our house. All of you.

    They go, except for DE KNOP.

DE KNOP. This is my house. You people've ruined this country. You get out of my house. Or I will burn you out.

MANIK. Out, comrade.

    DE KNOP *goes.*

SINGER. Manik. Otto. My friend. Would you please go and talk to Stefan for me? If he hasn't already gone – please, God – could Stefan Gutman please give Peter Singer five minutes more.

MANIK *goes.* SINGER *opens* STEFAN's *letter.*

SINGER. 'Peter, if only I'd had a talent for painting as big as your talent for life – '. That's true, Stefan, but I've had practice. You've only had one life. I've had five so far. The first ended in a cattle truck, the second in the joy of liberation, the third in water, the fourth in a tea party in this room. The fifth life, which nearly choked itself to death on a halo, ended with an invitation to lunch. Five lives, some better than others. Now I'm starting a sixth. No. No. I'm going back to the first of all. The one I thought I'd left behind in a railway car. You were right, Stefan. It wasn't a mistake to remember. The mistake was not remembering enough.

He reads some more.

'Remember you had a true friend who always loved you. Burn the canvasses for me. Remember me as I was in Lvov. Imagine what I might have been. Forget what I became. Stefan.' Stefan?

MANIK *comes back carrying* STEFAN's *body, bloody, his wrists cut open. He sets him down and weeps.*

Stefan? Don't let a single death be the end of you. If you can't live, then how can I?

A crash, below. The sound of fire.

DE KNOP (*off*). Singer!

MANIK. We should go, Peter. Go now.

He helps SINGER *into his old overcoat.* SINGER *kisses* STEFAN.

SINGER. Sleep, Stefan, sleep for a hundred years, or wake with no memory. But if you wake soon and remember any of this, all I can tell you is: there is no way in the world of forgetting what you love and what you fear.

MANIK. Peter. Time now.

They start to climb to the roof.

SINGER. When someone builds a machine the size of half a continent, employing a cast of thousands, just to make you into soap, it's hard to take entirely seriously the idea of progress. But it's necessary to go on trying.

They escape through the roof.

Epilogue

Enter CHORUS, *taking off his rags.*

CHORUS. There was a terrible truth inside that vast Wagnerian machine. It was truly the world's most convincing soap opera. For though the audience by and large heartily disapproved, the players couldn't help believing that the play was real. Were the dumplings in Manik's dreams real? Yes. Because he was careful only to dream of real dumplings. And so, in our way, without an army or a great machine, we've played for real too. Have we told the truth? Yes. Have we told the whole truth? No. We were careful not to. For this is a theatre, in which there's always so much else to say. If we had all night. And another day.

Exit.

The End.